Songs of Shabkar

Songs of Shabkar

The Path of a Tibetan Yogi Inspired by Nature

Translations & Photographs
by Victoria Sujata

DHARMA PUBLISHING

TIBETAN TRANSLATION SERIES

1. Calm and Clear
2. The Legend of the Great Stupa
3. Mind in Buddhist Psychology
4. Golden Zephyr (Nāgārjuna)
5. Kindly Bent to Ease Us, Parts 1–3
6. Elegant Sayings (Nāgārjuna, Sakya Paṇḍita)
7. The Life and Liberation of Padmasambhava
8. Buddha's Lions: Lives of the 84 Siddhas
9. The Voice of the Buddha (Lalitavistara Sūtra)
10. The Marvelous Companion (Āryaśūra's Jātakamālā)
11. Mother of Knowledge: Enlightenment of Yeshe Tshogyal
12. The Dhammapada (Teachings on 26 Topics)
13. The Fortunate Aeon (Bhadrakalpika Sūtra)
14. Master of Wisdom (Nāgārjuna)
15. Joy for the World (Candrakīrti)
16. Wisdom of Buddha (Saṁdhinirmocana Sūtra)
17. Path of Heroes: Birth of Enlightenment
18. Gathering the Meanings (The Arthaviniścaya Sūtra)
19. Invitation to Enlightenment (Mātṛceṭa & Candragomin)
20. Leaves of the Heaven Tree (Collection of 108 Jātakas)
21. Songs of Shabkar: The Path of a Tibetan Yogi Inspired by Nature

Produced under the auspices of the Yeshe De Project.
Printed in the U.S.A. at Dharma Mangalam Press, Ratna Ling.

ISBN: 978-0-89800-000-9
Library of Congress Control Number: 2010941162

10 9 8 7 6 5 4 3 2 1

www.dharmapublishing.com

In memory of

the incomparable

E. Gene Smith (1936–2010),

whose kindness is impossible to repay

Contents

Publisher's Preface

Shabkar Tshogdruk Rangdrol was a great yogin and practitioner of both Nyingma and Sarma teachings in the *rimey* tradition. A master poet and skilled writer, he sang beautiful songs and authored many texts on practice. Deeply experienced in *Madhyamaka, Mahāmudra,* and *Dzogpa Chenpo,* he possessed both learned understanding and yogic achievement, while his conduct was similar to that of Jetsün Milarepa. Throughout Tibet he was renowned as an example of the finest practitioner. The great Patrul Rinpoche deeply admired Shabkar and wished to meet him, though the opportunity never arose.

Dharma Publishing is pleased to have this opportunity to publish a collection of Shabkar's songs. These songs were his special way of teaching, reflecting his profound understanding and his way of life. Sincere practitioners should read with great care and awareness to contact the depth of meaning conveyed in each song. Listen to the words and let them resonate within you, until they point directly to your life and your mind. In this way, you can explore the Dharma from the inside, glimpsing the way of life of a true practitioner. This is Shabkar's precious gift to us today.

Tarthang Tulku
Founder of Dharma Publishing
Odiyan Fall, 2010

Translator's Preface

Tshogdruk Rangdrol (1781–1851), or Shabkar, as many people call him, is already known in the West by the lovely translation of his autobiography by M. Ricard,[1] which has many songs in it. Translations from another rich source of songs by this yogi from Amdo,[2] *The Festival of Melodious Songs*,[3] have been almost exclusively unpublished. I have chosen fifty songs from this vast collection to present here.

The songs of spiritual realization, known as *gur*, are a genre of unique importance for understanding the tradition of Tibetan Buddhism. They have religious themes but are at the same time more direct expressions of personal experience than classic monastic literature with its biographies, histories, philosophical instruction, and instruction on meditation and deities. *Gur* are sung largely by recluses in solitude or for other hermit-disciples away from monastic settings; their expression is often less formal and very personal. Because they show not only the highest levels that a saint attains but also the low points, bawdy humor, and inner struggles along the path, they provide road maps for others to follow that make enlightenment seem attainable by anyone who will renounce the world and do spiritual practices in solitude. Because *gur* are simple expressions of personal religious insights that aim to appeal to the people in a way that is accessible and pleasing, they fill an essential role in Tibetan Buddhism.

Gur are also unique in terms of style. On the one hand, they can show considerable folk influence in metrics and figures of speech, and their melodies are probably related to folk melodies, like those of their forerunners, the songs of the *mahāsiddhas*, in India. Yet at the same time *gur* are not simply spiritually themed folk songs; they can also be influenced by very formal Indian classical verse, especially if their author at one time studied in a monastery. In that way, they can be an intriguing blend of classical and folk, formal and informal, foreign and indigenous.[4]

Finding myself irresistibly drawn to the *gur* of Shabkar because of his depth and richness of personal expression in very simple styles, I have chosen less formal forms of *gur* for this collection of translations, songs that are outspoken in terms of opinions and feelings. Shabkar is often concerned with themes such as the importance of confronting the inescapability of death, and the spontaneous development of spiritual qualities and happiness that comes about when one renounces the world and lives in a pleasing solitary place. With delightful lightheartedness and clarity, he expresses criticism, often scathingly, of himself, other clergy, and the evils of his homeland and village monastery. He expresses feelings of sadness at the loss of his parents and the inescapability of impermanence, longing for his lama, and anger over the absence of virtue. He describes his lifestyle, and tells us why he chose to live in hermitages, and why he sings *gur*. And he expresses spiritual ideas in very simple, experiential ways. There is surely a place for gorgeous hagiographies of realized masters, but here one finds what Shabkar said about himself, and so we can see the stages he went through and learn that at many points in his life, he was actually quite similar to us. While the more formal *gur*, characterized by rich styles adhering to the rules of poetics—or *kāvya*—that originated in the fifth century in India, are certainly beautiful in their ornateness, the *gur* I have translated here are less complex. I hope that the reader will find them beautiful in their own right.

Shabkar often made analogies from nature—leaves, flowers, lakes, clouds, snow-covered mountains, sun, and animals—to express spiritual ideas in the simplest terms possible to himself or other mountain hermits. On the surface, the descriptions may seem absurdly simple:

Rain and snow both
Hurt my head.
I could not block each drop and flake.
I benefited by wearing a hat.

Stones and thorns both
Hurt my feet.
I could not avoid each stone and thorn.
I benefited by wearing shoes.

But I find that his simple, outspoken expressions cut right to the point in an unforgettable way:

> Lies and harsh words both
> Hurt my mind.
> I was not able to reply to each lie and insult.
> I benefited from meditating on forgiveness.[5]

The benefits one can gain from practicing religion are as concrete and direct as the benefits one gains from wearing a hat or shoes. While there's unequivocally a place for the very valuable, long, complex philosophical commentaries that are the hallmark of much of Tibetan Buddhist literature, these simple songs fill another role and sometimes resonate very quickly and directly with the very core of our sense of truth.

I have organized the collection of *gur* I present here around thirteen topics. The central theme is the attainment of realization, but this is best done in a hermitage, and a hermitage is of no use if one has not renounced the world, an act itself inspired by confronting impermanence and death. So spiritual development involves layers, and I have ordered my themes around the process that Shabkar himself tells us he followed to attain experiences of realization.[6]

I start with a chapter with songs about lamas, since the lama is regarded as the source of all one's blessings and benefits in Tibetan Buddhism. My next theme is impermanence, since the realization that things are always changing and lack inherent existence is meant to inspire one to take advantage of one's human body in times of youth and health to practice the Dharma. Pain over the passing away of parents deepens one's awareness of impermanence, and reminds one of lost opportunities. Chapter four is about nature, where Shabkar tells us he sees lessons in the clouds, sun, and wind; and recalls his lama when he looks at the trees, birds, and sky. My fifth theme is death, since Shabkar says that confronting the reality of the inescapability of death will inspire one to the Dharma in this lifetime, while one has a human body. We are told that once the yogi has prepared fully, "although the point of death has arrived, he has no regrets." Chapter six is devoted to renunciation, because without renunciation, one will have impediments to one's practice and one's happiness.

Chapter seven has songs about old age. But now, having renounced concerns of this world, old age is depicted as a time of great joy in which one is able to bring limitless benefit to beings. Chapter eight contains a *gur* on self-criticism, something rarely encountered in Tibetan literature. Although viewed as highly realized by others, Shabkar is quick to express his faults with great disdain. He concludes that he should get away from both the village and the monastery, where his behavior is bad, and go to a solitary grove. My next chapter deals with nonsectarianism, where the teachings of *Dzogchen*, *Mahāmudrā*, and *Madhyamaka*, and the teachers Padmasaṃbhava, Milarepa, and Tsongkhapa are presented with equally high respect.

Chapter ten has songs about hermitages, where Shabkar says one is out of danger from the "blazing pit" of one's homeland and can practice well, and be spontaneously happy. Chapter eleven is on the wonderful meditation experiences that one can have in solitary places, and includes instructions on *Dzogchen*, given in terms of metaphors from nature. Chapter twelve is about the happiness that Shabkar says one will spontaneously feel, having renounced the world and being in mountain hermitages. He tells us, "Yogis who die like deer are happy." And chapter thirteen is about what he himself says about singing *gur*—how it is an excellent way of expounding the Dharma and benefits the minds of others, and how it honors the deities. Singing *gur* is a yogi's realized nature. To enhance the readers' experiences of the songs, I provide some sixty color photos of my own, all taken in Amdo where I have lived most summers since 1993. I have chosen photos that complement the themes of their respective chapters.

It is with pleasure that I present my second book on *gur*. My translations are less literal than my previous ones, since my primary intention here is to communicate what Shabkar is telling us, so I go beyond a simple stringing together of definitions from the still highly limited dictionaries. On the other hand, I have not enhanced the language in an attempt to make the *gur* something that they are not. This was not out of an obsession with scholarship or blind faith on my part, but out of a recognition that the *gur* are already powerful expressions of spiritual experiences and realization.

It is my hope that this book will be enjoyed by scholars in Tibetan and Buddhist studies, as well as newcomers, so I have made my translations accessible to the novice reader by spelling the proper names and other Tibetan words phonetically, and by explaining technical Buddhist terms in the glossary. Scholars in the field will realize that the rich Tibetan meters[7] cannot be duplicated in translation, but I have included my sources here, so that those with a knowledge of Tibetan can enjoy the songs in their original language at leisure.

Victoria Sujata, Ph.D.
Boston and Rebgong
2010

Notes

1 Zhabs dkar Tshogs drug rang grol, 1781–1851, *The Life of Shabkar: The Autobiography of a Tibetan Yogin*, trans. Matthieu Ricard, et al. (Albany: State University of New York Press, 1994). This is a translation of the first part of his autobiography (henceforth referred to as *SH*). *See* Zhabs dkar Tshogs drug rang grol, *Snyigs dus 'gro ba yongs kyi skyabs mgon zhabs dkar rdo rje 'chang chen po'i rnam par thar pa rgyas par bshad pa skal bzang gdul bya thar 'dod rnams kyi re ba skong ba'i yid bzhin gyi nor bu bsam 'phel dbang gi rgyal po*, in *Rje zhabs dkar tshogs drug rang grol gyi gsung 'bum* by Zhabs dkar Tshogs drug rang grol, vol. 1 (Xining: Mtsho sngon mi rigs dpe skrun khang, 2002). This edition will henceforth be referred to as *ZH*.

2 Shabkar is from Rebgong in the region of Amdo, on the northeastern side of the Tibetan plateau. *See* maps 1 and 2.

3 Zhabs dkar Tshogs drug rang grol, [*Bya btang tshogs drug rang grol gyis rang dang skal ldan gdul bya la mgrin pa gdams pa'i bang mdzod nas glu dbyangs dga' ston 'gyed pa rnams*], in *Rje zhabs dkar tshogs drug rang grol gyi gsung 'bum*, vols. 3–4 (Xining: Mtsho sngon mi rigs dpe skrun khang, 2002). These volumes will henceforth be referred to as Zhabs dkar, *Gsung 'bum* 3 and Zhabs dkar, *Gsung 'bum* 4. Unfortunately, there is no title given for the collection of *gur* in this edition, but since the title is found in other editions (such as the Shechen publication of 2003 in my bibliography), I have assumed that it is missing, and have inserted it here in brackets. I thank the late E.G. Smith for his advice in this regard.

Shabkar (= Zhabs dkar) preserved in writing many of the songs he had sung, and it seems likely that when he was composing his autobiography—which alternates between songs and narration—he chose from a vast number of songs already written. Those he did not use in his autobiography were compiled into collections of his songs, the sources I am using here. For this see *SH*, xix, 579.

4 For brief descriptions of the genre of *gur*'s predecessors in India, the *caryāgīti* and *dohā*, and the development of *gur* in Tibet up through the sixteenth century, see V. Sujata, *Tibetan Songs of Realization*, 78–85. For a discussion of poetic figures that appear in *gur* that are influenced by very formal Indian classical verse, and ones that are indigenously Tibetan, see V. Sujata, *Tibetan Songs of Realization*, 162–246.

5 Zhabs dkar, *Gsung 'bum* 4: 480–81.

6 *See,* for example, the first song in the chapter on meditation experiences.

7 For a detailed discussion of the Tibetan use of metrics, the backbone of verse, see V. Sujata, *Tibetan Songs of Realization*, 112–38.

Acknowledgements

I can never express enough gratitude to the many people who have either helped me arrive at the point of being able to compile and translate this collection of *gur*, or who have contributed to it more directly. A number of monks and lay people in the Rebgong area of Amdo, where I have been living for most summers since 1993, have contributed to this book in crucial ways. I could not have completed my translations without the consistent and expert assistance of one of the great scholars of Rebgong, Lobzang Chödrag (or Chidrag, in the local dialect), who patiently answered all the questions I posed regarding my translations, and tirelessly sorted out questions of spelling in the sources. I would also like to thank Akhu Paljor (Akhö Whanjor), Gendun Trinley, and Lobzang Tashi for their wisdom, inspiration, hospitality, and laughter.

In the West, I want to first thank Dharma Publishing for accepting my manuscript for publication, and Arnaud Maitland, the director, for enthusiastically supporting this project. In particular, I wish to express gratitude to Leslie Bradburn, senior editor and researcher for the Yeshe De Project, for her countless hours of care to make sure the translations and glossary here meet the high spiritual standards of Dharma Publishing, and Eric Brandebury, the prepress manager, for having handled all the technical aspects of producing my photographs beautifully. Chris Leahy of the Massachusetts Audubon Society gave me much crucial information regarding the names and songs of the birds in the *gur* translated here. K.E. Duffin, formerly of the Writing Center at Harvard, read the entire manuscript and offered many insightful suggestions that helped bring out Shabkar's intentions. C. Scott Walker, of the Harvard Map Collection, worked with me meticulously to produce the maps that I wanted. The incomparable

E. Gene Smith of The Tibetan Buddhist Resource Center, Professor Leonard van der Kuijp of Harvard University, Ronnie Broadfoot of Harvard's Museum of Comparative Zoology, and Erik Pema Kunsang of Rangjung Yeshe Publications generously offered advice about lingering details. I owe much gratitude to my teachers of Tibetan language, culture, and history at Harvard from 1989 to 2003, the late Michael Aris, who fanned the embers of my fascination with Tibetology; and L. van der Kuijp, who offered many invaluable suggestions regarding my thesis on *gur,* and with whom I first translated some songs of Shabkar. Many other people in my life have contributed to the creation of this book in their own ways, especially Laurel McGregor, Nancy Barrett, Louis Belden, Jim Haskins, Roger Tawa, and Yang Chengcai, and I thank them all for their persistent encouragement and support. I accept responsibility for any remaining mistakes in this book.

Translations

Chapter One

Lamas

སྙིང་སྟོང་སང་ནམ་མཁའ་ཡངས་པ་ལ།།
དངུལ་མདོག་འདྲའི་ན་བུན་ཡངས་པ་བཞིན།།
ཕྱོགས་ཀུན་ཁྱབ་ནམ་མཁའི་ཀློང་ཡངས་ནས།།
རྗེ་བླ་མའི་གཟུགས་སྐུ་བསྟན་ན་ཨང་།།

མདོག་རབ་མཛེས་འཇའ་ཚོན་རི་མོ་འཕེན།།
ཆར་འཇམ་པོ་དལ་བུར་བབས་པ་བཞིན།།
འཇའ་འོད་ལྔའི་གུར་ཁྱིམ་ཞིག་ནང་ནས།།
ཆོས་ཟབ་མོ་མང་པོ་གསུངས་ན་ཨང་།།

ས་བདེ་འཇམ་ཡངས་པའི་སྤང་གཞོངས་སུ།།
ཆར་ཧི་བབས་སྙིང་དུ་འཁྱིལ་བ་བཞིན།།
སེམས་དང་གུས་ཆེ་བའི་སློབ་བུ་ངས།།
ཆོས་གང་གསུངས་ཡིད་ལ་བཟུང་ན་ཨང་།།

མདོག་རབ་མཛེས་མེ་ཏོག་སྣ་ཚོགས་པ།།
སྤང་བདེ་འཇམ་སྙིང་དུ་སྐྱེ་བ་བཞིན།།
ཉམས་རྟོགས་པའི་ཡོན་ཏན་སྣ་ཚོགས་པ།།
བུ་བདག་གི་རྒྱུད་ལ་སྐྱེས་ན་ཨང་།།

ཞེས་པ་འདི་ཡང་ཉིན་ཞིག་ཕྱིའི་སྣང་བས་རྐྱེན་བྱས་ནས་བླངས་པའོ།།

Like the silver mist that rises
In the wide, empty sky,
The bodily form of the lord lama has revealed itself
In that vast expanse encompassing all directions. Hey!

Like gentle rain that slowly falls,
Drawing out the colorful bands of a beautiful rainbow,
He has expounded many deep teachings
From within a canopy of rainbow-colored light. Hey!

Like rainwater that falls and forms puddles
On the soil of a soft, wide, grassy meadow,
Whatever teachings the lama has expounded,
I am their vessel, a disciple of great faith and respect. Hey!

Like the many kinds of flowers with beautiful colors
That bloom in a soft meadow,
A variety of profound experiences and realization
Have arisen in my mind-stream, because I am your spiritual son. Hey!

I also sang this, feeling inspired by external appearances one day.

རྒྱལ་བའི་བསྟན་པ་རིན་པོ་ཆེ།།
འཛིན་སྐྱོང་སྤེལ་བའི་ཐུགས་རྗེ་ཅན།།
དགེ་དབང་བློ་བཟང་བསྟན་འཛིན་ལ།།
གསོལ་བ་འདེབས་སོ་བྱིན་གྱིས་རློབས།།

ཕ་མ་གཉིས་ཀྱིས་གཅེས་ཕྲུག་དེ།།
ཆུང་དུས་བརྩེ་བས་སྐྱོང་བ་ལྟར།།
མཚན་ལྡན་བླ་མ་བཟང་པོ་ཡིས།།
སྣོད་ལྡན་སློབ་བུ་དེ་ལྟར་སྐྱོངས།།

རྩལ་ལྡན་སེང་གེ་དཀར་མོ་ཡིས།།
སེང་ཕྲུག་ཆུང་དུས་སྐྱོང་བ་ལྟར།།
མཚན་ལྡན་བླ་མ་བཟང་པོ་ཡིས།།
སྣོད་ལྡན་སློབ་བུ་དེ་ལྟར་སྐྱོངས།།

བྱ་རྒྱལ་ཁང་དཀར་རྒོད་པོ་ཡིས།།
རྒོད་ཕྲུག་ཆུང་དུས་སྐྱོང་བ་ལྟར།།
མཚན་ལྡན་བླ་མ་བཟང་པོ་ཡིས།།
སྣོད་ལྡན་སློབ་བུ་དེ་ལྟར་སྐྱོངས།།

I pray to Ngawang Lobzang Tendzin,
The compassionate one, who upholds, preserves, and spreads
The precious teachings of the Victorious Ones.
Please bless me.

Just as parents protect their beloved children
With affection when they are small,
Likewise, kind, qualified lama,
Please protect your worthy disciples.

Just as powerful white lionesses
Protect their cubs,
Likewise, kind, qualified lama,
Please protect your worthy disciples.

Just as the royal white vultures
Protect their chicks,
Likewise, kind, qualified lama,
Please protect your worthy disciples.

ཏྭ་སྟོན་བྲི་སེར་འབྲོང་པོ་ཡིས།།
འབྲོང་ཞུག་ཆུང་དུས་སྐྱོང་བ་ལྟར།།
མཚན་ལྡན་བླ་མ་བཟང་པོ་ཡིས།།
སྣོད་ལྡན་སློབ་བུ་དེ་ལྟར་སྐྱོངས།།

སྨན་པ་ཤིན་ཏུ་མཁས་པ་ཡིས།།
ནད་པ་བརྩེ་བས་སྐྱོང་བ་ལྟར།།
མཚན་ལྡན་བླ་མ་བཟང་པོ་ཡིས།།
སྣོད་ལྡན་སློབ་བུ་དེ་ལྟར་སྐྱོངས།།

ཆོས་དང་ཟང་ཟིང་གཉིས་ཀ་ལ།།
ཕངས་པ་མེད་པར་སློབ་བུ་སྐྱོངས།།
ཚེ་འདི་ཕྱི་མ་བར་དོ་གསུམ།།
གང་དུ་བརྩེ་བས་སློབ་བུ་སྐྱོངས།།

གླུ་འདི་ཚོགས་དྲུག་རང་གྲོལ་བླངས།།
འདི་ཉིད་ཐོས་ཚད་ཐམས་ཅད་ཀྱིས།།
སྣོད་དང་ལྡན་པའི་སློབ་མ་རྣམས།།
ཆོས་བཞིན་བརྩེ་བས་སྐྱོང་བར་ཤོག།

Just as wild, blue-horned yaks
Protect their calves,
Likewise, kind, qualified lama,
Please protect your worthy disciples.

Just as highly skilled doctors
Protect their patients with love,
Likewise, kind, qualified lama,
Please protect your worthy disciples.

Please care for your spiritual sons
Both spiritually and materially, without hesitation.
Wherever we are in this life, the next, or in the *bardo,*
Please protect your spiritual sons with love.

Tshogdruk Rangdrol sang this song.
May all those who heard it
Lovingly protect their worthy disciples
In accordance with the Dharma.

རྩལ་ལྡན་དར་སེང་ཕྲུ་གུ་རྣམས།།
གངས་དཀར་ལྟེངས་སུ་བདེ་བར་བཞུད།།
སླར་ཡང་དར་སེང་ཕྲུ་གུ་རྣམས།།
ཡང་དང་ཡང་དུ་འཕྲད་པར་ཤོག།

འདབ་བཟང་བྱ་རྒོད་ཕྲུ་གུ་རྣམས།།
དགུང་སྔོན་མཁའ་ལ་བདེ་བར་བཞུད།།
སླར་ཡང་བྱ་རྒོད་ཕྲུ་གུ་རྣམས།།
ཡང་དང་ཡང་དུ་འཕྲད་པར་ཤོག།

དཔའ་བོ་རྒྱ་སྟག་ཕྲུ་གུ་རྣམས།།
ཙན་དན་ནགས་ལ་བདེ་བར་བཞུད།།
སླར་ཡང་རྒྱ་སྟག་ཕྲུ་གུ་རྣམས།།
ཡང་དང་ཡང་དུ་འཕྲད་པར་ཤོག།

བྱ་བཏང་བདག་གི་སློབ་བུ་རྣམས།།
རི་བོ་རྩེ་ལྷུར་བདེ་བར་བཞུད།།
སླར་ཡང་རྣལ་འབྱོར་དཔོན་སློབ་རྣམས།།
ཡང་དང་ཡང་དུ་འཕྲད་པར་ཤོག།

The cubs of the powerful snow lioness
Are merrily heading off to the summit of the snow mountain.
May the snow lioness and her cubs
Meet again later, again and again.

The chicks of the vulture with powerful wings
Are merrily heading off into the blue sky.
May the vulture and her chicks
Meet again later, again and again.

The cubs of the courageous tigress
Are merrily heading off to the sandalwood forest.
May the tigress and her cubs
Meet again later, again and again.

The disciples of this renunciant
Are merrily heading off to Wutaishan.
May the yogi master and you disciples
Meet again later, again and again.

རྩ་བརྒྱུད་བླ་མའི་བྱིན་རླབས་དང་།།
ཡི་དམ་ལྷ་ཡི་ཐུགས་རྗེ་དང་།།
མཁའ་འགྲོ་ཆོས་སྐྱོང་མཐུ་སྟོབས་ཀྱིས།།
སྨོན་པ་བཞིན་དུ་འགྲུབ་གྱུར་ཅིག།

ཅེས་པ་འདི་ཡང་སློབ་བུ་ཐུབ་བསྟན་རྒྱ་མཚོ་སོགས་ཁ་ཤས་རི་བོ་རྩེ་ལྔར་འགྲོ་བའི་ཚེ་ཚོགས་དྲུག་རང་གྲོལ་གྱིས་འགྲོ་རྫོངས་སུ་བླངས་པའོ།།

Through the blessings of the root and lineage lamas,

The compassion of *yidam*s and deities,

And the power and strength of the *ḍākinī*s and *dharmapāla*s,

May you fulfill your aspirations.

Tshogdruk Rangdrol sang this as a farewell gift, when Thubten Gyatso and several other disciples were going off to Wutaishan.

ཤ་རྒྱུད་རི་དྭགས་རྣམས་རྩེ་བའི་རི་ཁྲོད་ཀྱི།།
ལྗོན་ཤིང་མེ་ཏོག་རྣམས་མཛོང་བས་རྒྱན་བྱས་ནས།།
དྲིན་ཅན་བླ་མ་ཡི་གཟུགས་སྐུ་ཡིད་ལ་ཤར།།
ཡང་ཡང་མཇལ་རྒྱུ་ཞིག་བྱུང་ན་དགའ་བ་ལ།།

ཡིད་མཐུན་བག་ཕབ་ཀྱི་བྱ་རིགས་སྣ་ཚོགས་པའི།།
སྐད་སྙན་གྲག་པ་དེ་ཐོས་པས་རྒྱན་བྱས་ནས།།
དྲིན་ཅན་བླ་མ་ཡི་གསུང་དབྱངས་ཡིད་ལ་ཤར།།
ཡང་ཡང་མཇལ་རྒྱུ་ཞིག་བྱུང་ན་དགའ་བ་ལ།།

མཐོ་ཞིང་ཡངས་པ་ཡི་སྤྲིན་མེད་ལྷ་ལམ་གྱི།།
ཉིམ་གཞོན་ནུ་དེ་མཛོང་བས་རྒྱན་བྱས་ནས།།
དྲིན་ཅན་བླ་མ་ཡི་མཁྱེན་བརྩེ་ཡིད་ལ་ཤར།།
ཡང་ཡང་མཇལ་རྒྱུ་ཞིག་བྱུང་ན་དགའ་བ་ལ།།

ཞེས་པ་འདི་ཡང་ཉིན་ཞིག་ཆོས་རྒྱལ་ངག་གི་དབང་པོའི་ཞབས་པད་བསྟེན་དུས། སྐུའི་དབྱིབས་གསུང་གི་གདངས་ཐུགས་རྗེས་བསྐྱངས་ཚུལ་རྣམས་ཡིད་ལ་ཤར་ཚེ་ཚོགས་དྲུག་རང་གྲོལ་གྱིས་སྨྲས་པའོ།།

Because I saw trees and flowers
At a mountain hermitage where deer, asses, and other hoofed
animals play,
The bodily form of my kind lama came to mind.
If only I could meet him again—Oh joy!

Because I heard all kinds of friendly, carefree birds
Calling out sweetly,
The melodious speech of my kind lama came to mind.
If only I could meet him over and over—Oh happiness!

Because I saw the sun rise
Into the high, broad, cloudless sky,
The wisdom and compassion of my kind lama came to mind.
If only I could be in his presence again and again—Oh delight!

I expressed this one day during a period in which I was serving at the lotus feet of my lama, Chögyäl Ngakyi Wangpo, when the form of my lama's body, his melodious speech, and the way the lama compassionately cared for me came to mind.

Chapter Two

Impermanence

ན་མོ་གུ་རུ།

སྦྲང་ཆར་འཛམ་པོ་འབབ་ཅིང་ཆུ་བྲུས་སྐད་སྙན་སྒྲོག།
སྣ་ཚོགས་མེ་ཏོག་གཡོ་ཞིང་བུང་བ་སྒྲ་བཅས་འཁོར།།
དུས་མི་རིང་བར་མི་མཐུན་ཁ་རླུང་འཚུབ་པ་ཡིས།།
ས་གཞི་སྐྱ་བོར་གཏོང་བའི་ཚུལ་ལ་བསམ་ཞིང་སྐྱོ།།

དུས་ཀྱི་འགྱུར་ལྡོག་དེ་བཞིན་ད་ལྟའི་གནས་སྐབས་འདིར།།
ལུས་ལ་ནད་མེད་སྨྲ་ཨུ་བདེ་ཞིང་བློ་གསལ་ཡང་།།
དུས་མི་རིང་བར་མི་མཐུན་ན་ཚ་འཆི་བ་ཡིས།།
བཅོམ་ནས་འཇིག་རྟེན་ཕ་རོལ་འགྲོ་ཚུལ་བསམ་ཞིང་སྐྱོ།།

ཞེས་པ་འདི་ནི་ཚོགས་དྲུག་རང་གྲོལ་གྱིས་ཉིན་ཞིག་སེམས་ལ་སྐྱོ་ཤས་ཐན་ཐུན་སྐྱེས་པའི་ཚེ་བླངས་པའོ།།

I bow to the guru.

A soft, pleasant rain is falling and waterbirds are calling ardently.
Flowers are waving and bees are buzzing around.
But before long, things will not be harmonious.
Thinking about the way blizzards will pummel the earth
    and leave it white,
I feel disillusioned.

Right now my body is not ill,
I am articulate, and my mind is clear.
But just as the seasons change, soon things will not be harmonious.
Thinking about the way sickness, old age, and death will
    pummel me,
And I will pass beyond this world,
I feel disillusioned.

I, Tshogdruk Rangdrol, sang this one day when I felt a little sad.

ན་མོ་གུ་རུ།

མགོ་དང་དོན་སྙིང་འདྲ་བའི།།
བླ་མ་ཆོས་ཀྱི་རྒྱལ་པོ།།
རིག་འཛིན་འཇམ་དབྱངས་རྒྱ་མཚོ།།
དག་པའི་ཞིང་དུ་ག་ཤེགས་ཐལ།།

ཡན་ལག་ཉིང་ལག་འདྲ་བའི།།
ཕ་མ་མཆེད་གྲོགས་ཡོན་བདག།
ལ་ལ་ཤི་བྲལ་བྱས་སོང་།།
ལ་ལ་གསོན་བྲལ་བྱས་ཐལ།།

མི་མེད་ལུང་བ་སྟོང་བའི།།
བྲག་ཁུང་སྙམ་པོའི་ནང་དུ།།
བན་རྐན་རང་ཉིད་གཅིག་པུར།།
གཟུགས་ཕུང་བཞིན་དུ་ལུས་ཐལ།།

ཚུལ་དེ་ཞིབ་ཏུ་བསམས་ཚེ།།
སྐྱོ་ཤས་ཤུགས་དྲག་སྐྱེ་ནས།།
མིག་ནས་མཆི་མའི་ཐིགས་པ།།
མ་ཟུང་འཁག་རེ་ཤོར་ཐལ།།

I bow to the guru.

My lama Chökyi Gyälpo,
And the knowledge holder Jamyang Gyatso,
Who are like my head and heart,
Have gone to Pure Realms.

And parents, spiritual friends, and patrons,
Who are like my arms and fingers—
Some have died
And some have gone away.

I myself, an old monk, am alone
In a dry cave
In this uninhabited valley.
I have been left behind like a human corpse.

When I thought more closely about my situation,
Intense disillusionment arose.
I did not hold back my teardrops,
And some stole away.

ད་ནི་མ་གྱུར་འགྲོ་བའི།།
དོན་དུ་བྱང་ཆུབ་སེམས་བསྐྱེད།།
རི་ཁྲོད་དབེན་པའི་གནས་སུ།།
ཚེ་དང་སྒྲུབ་པ་སྙོམས་ཡ།།

རང་གཞན་གཉིས་ཀ་འཚོངས་པའི།།
བྱང་ཆུབ་གོ་འཕང་ཐོབ་ན།།
བྱ་བཏང་པ་ངའི་དགའ་བ།།
རི་ཁྲོད་པ་ངའི་སྐྱིད་པ།།

ཞེས་པ་འདི་ཡང་ཚོགས་དྲུག་རང་གྲོལ་གྱིས་གླངས་པའོ།།

But I am now generating *bodhicitta* in this mountain hermitage
For the sake of all sentient beings—
My mothers in past lives.
May the length of my practice equal the length of my life! Hey!

If I attain enlightenment
For the sake of my fulfillment and that of others,
I, a renunciant, will rejoice.
I, a mountain hermit, will be happy.

Tshogdruk Rangdrol sang this also.

Chapter Three

Passing Away of Mother and Father

ཧེ་བླ་མ་སངས་རྒྱས་སྤྱི་བོར་བཞུགས།།
སྤྱིར་མ་གྱུར་འགྲོ་ལ་ཐུགས་རྗེས་གཟིགས།།
སྒོས་ཨ་མའི་སྐྱིད་སྡུག་ཁྱེད་རང་མཁྱེན།།

ང་ཨ་མར་ལན་གཅིག་འཕྲད་སྙམ་འོང་།།
མ་མ་འཕྲད་ཤི་བའི་རྨུས་པ་འཕྲད།།
ངས་བསམ་ཞིང་ཨ་མ་དྲན་ནས་བྱུང་།།

གཏམ་སྙན་མོ་བཤད་སྙམ་བསྒྲིགས་ནས་འོང་།།
གཏམ་བཤད་ཡུལ་ཨ་མ་ཤི་བཙོས།།
ངས་བསམ་ཞིང་ཨ་མ་དྲན་ནས་བྱུང་།།

ལུས་འཕྲད་འདོད་རེ་བ་སུ་ཡིས་སྐོང་།།
གཏམ་ཚིག་འགའ་ཡོད་པ་སུ་ལ་སྨྲ།།
ངས་བསམ་ཞིང་ཨ་མ་དྲན་ནས་བྱུང་།།

ཡུལ་ཁང་ཆུང་སྒོ་ཡི་ཕྱི་ནང་ན།།
སྔོན་ཨ་མ་ཡོད་ཚུལ་ཡིད་ལ་ཤར།།
ངས་བསམ་ཞིང་ཨ་མ་དྲན་ནས་བྱུང་།།

Lord lama—Buddha—please dwell on my crown *cakra*.
Please watch compassionately over all sentient beings, who
have been my mothers in other lives.
In particular, my current mother's fate is now in your hands.

When it occurred to me to go see my mother one more time,
I could not meet her. Instead I met her bones.
When I think of mother, I miss her so.

I thought I would make an eloquent speech,
prepared it, and have come to your house.
The reason for my speech—dear departed mother—listen!
When I think of mother, I miss her so.

Who will satisfy a son's longing and hope to meet his mother again?
To whom will I deliver the few words I have prepared?
When I think of mother, I miss her so.

The way mother would be standing there
By the front door of our small home comes back to me.
When I think of mother, I miss her so.

མ་བཟང་མོའི་ལུས་དབྱིབས་རྣམ་འགྱུར་དང་།།
དགའ་བ་ཤད་ཚུལ་ཡིད་ལ་ཡལ་ལེར་ཤར།།
ངས་བསམ་ཞིང་ཨ་མ་དྲན་ནས་བྱུང་།།

དུས་ད་ལྟ་ཡོད་ན་དགའ་བ་ལ།།
ང་བརྩེ་གདུང་སྒྲོ་ནས་འཕྲད་སྙིང་འདོད།།
ངས་བསམ་ཞིང་ཨ་མ་དྲན་ནས་བྱུང་།།

དུས་ད་ལྟ་ཡོད་ན་སྐྱིད་པ་ལ།།
གཏམ་སྙན་མོ་ཚིག་འགའ་བ་ཤད་སྙིང་འདོད།།
ངས་བསམ་ཞིང་ཨ་མ་དྲན་ནས་བྱུང་།།

ངེད་ཁ་སེམས་མཐུན་པའི་མ་བུ་གཉིས།།
ཚེ་འདི་རུམ་འཕྲད་ཞེ་རེ་འཕྲེད།།
ངས་བསམ་ཞིང་ཨ་མ་དྲན་ནས་བྱུང་།།

ཚེ་འདི་རུམ་འཕྲད་ཁོ་ཐག་ཆོད།།
ཚེ་ཕྱི་མར་འཕྲད་པའི་སྨོན་ལམ་འདེབས།།
ངས་བསམ་ཞིང་ཨ་མ་དྲན་ནས་བྱུང་།།

ད་བུ་ང་སྙིང་པོའི་ལྷ་ཆོས་བྱེད།།
རི་དབེན་པའི་དགའ་ཚལ་ཉམས་དགར་འགྲོ།།
ངས་བསམ་ཞིང་ཨ་མ་དྲན་ནས་བྱུང་།།

Mother's lovely form and manner,
And the way she would speak come vividly come to mind.
When I think of mother, I miss her so.

If she were still alive today—Oh joy!
With all my heart I really long to meet her.
When I think of mother, I miss her so.

If she were still alive today—Oh happiness!
My heart's desire is to speak a few sweet words to her.
When I think of mother, I miss her so.

Mother and son, whose minds and speech were as one—
Did not get to meet again in this life. What longing!
When I think of mother, I miss her so.

It has been determined: we shall not meet again in this life.
I pray that we meet in the next.
When I think of mother, I miss her so.

Now I, your son, am going off to a pleasing grove
of a mountain hermitage
To practice the essential, divine Dharma.
When I think of mother, I miss her so.

མགོན་སྐྱབས་གནས་བླ་མ་རྡོ་རྗེ་འཆང་།།
ངའི་ཨ་མ་ཐར་པའི་ལམ་ལ་དྲོངས།།
སྲུང་རི་ཁྲོད་ཟིན་པར་བྱིན་གྱིས་རློབས།།

ཞེས་སྨྲ་ངན་བྲུས།

Protector, place of refuge, lama—embodiment of the Buddhas—
Please guide my mother on the path of liberation.
Please give blessings to this beggar so he may keep to his
mountain retreat.

..... I lamented.

སྔོན་ཨ་མ་ཡོད་དུས་སྡུག་མི་འདོད།།
ད་སྡུག་ན་འདོད་དུས་ཨ་མ་མེད།།
དེ་གཉིས་ཀ་འཛོམ་པའི་དུས་མ་བྱུང་།།
ང་འདི་ནུ་མི་སྟོད་དབུས་སུ་འགྲོ།།

སྔོན་ཨ་མའི་དྲུང་ནས་འདུག་མ་འདོད།།
ད་བསྡད་ན་འདོད་དུས་ཨ་མ་མེད།།
དེ་གཉིས་ཀ་འཛོམ་པའི་དུས་མ་བྱུང་།།
ང་འདི་ནུ་མི་སྟོད་དབུས་སུ་འགྲོ།།

སྔོན་ཨ་མའི་ཚིག་ལ་ཉན་མ་འདོད།།
ད་ཉན་ན་འདོད་དུས་ཨ་མ་མེད།།
དེ་གཉིས་ཀ་འཛོམ་པའི་དུས་མ་བྱུང་།།
ང་འདི་ནུ་མི་སྟོད་དབུས་སུ་འགྲོ།།

རྗེ་མི་ལའི་སྒྲུབ་ཕུག་ལ་སོགས་སུ།།
ཆོས་ཟབ་མོ་ཚོལ་བཞིན་སྒྲུབ་ཏུ་འགྲོ།།
མི་ང་ཡི་རྗེས་འཇུག་བུ་སློབ་རྣམས།།
མི་ང་བཞིན་ཚེ་དང་སྒྲུབ་པ་སྙོམས།།

Before, when mother was alive, I did not want to see her.
Now, when I want to see her, mother is no more.
The time never came for us to meet again.
I won't stay here. I'm going to Ü.

Before, I did not want to be with mother.
Now, when I want to be with her, mother is no more.
The time never came for us to meet again.
I will not live here. I'm off to Ü.

Before, I would not listen to mother's words.
Now, when I want to hear them, mother is no more.
The time never came for us to meet again.
I won't remain here. I'm leaving for Ü.

I'm off to practice in accord with the deep Dharma
In the lord Milarepa's meditation cave, and similar places.
You followers and spiritual sons, do as I do:
May you practice as long as you live.

སྲུང་ང་ལ་བློ་གཏད་ཡོན་བདག་ཚོ།།
ལས་སྡིག་པ་སྤོངས་ལ་དགེ་བ་སྒྲུབས།།
ཀུན་ཚེ་རིང་ནད་མེད་ཆོས་མཐུན་སྒྲོས།།
སླར་ད་དུང་མཇལ་བའི་སྨོན་ལམ་འཚལ།།

ཞེས་བླངས་ནས་དབུས་གཙང་ཕྱོགས་སུ་ཆས་སོ།།

You patrons—trust in me, a wanderer.
Give up evil deeds and practice virtue!
Lead long, healthy lives and teach others in accord
with the Dharma.
And I pray we will meet again, at a later time.

Having sung this, I set out in the direction of Ütsang.

འཕགས་པ་ཐུགས་རྗེ་ཆེན་པོས་དགོངས་སུ་གསོལ།།
ཚེ་འདིར་དྲིན་གྱིས་བསྐྱངས་པའི་དྲིན་ཅན་ཕ།།
འཇིག་རྟེན་ཕྱི་མའི་ཡུལ་དུ་སོང་བ་ལ།།
གཡེལ་བ་མེད་པར་ཐུགས་རྗེས་སྤྱན་གྱིས་གཟིགས།།
ཤུལ་ནས་བུ་ཡིས་དཀོན་མཆོག་མཆོད་པ་དང་།།
དགེ་འདུན་བསྙེན་བཀུར་ལ་སོགས་དགེ་བའི་ལས།།
ཅི་བྱས་ཐམས་ཅད་མྱུར་དུ་རྗེས་འབྲངས་ནས།།
ཕྱི་མའི་དུས་སུ་ཕན་ཐོགས་འབྱུང་བར་ཤོག།

ཁྱིམ་ཚང་བཟའ་བའི་ཁ་རྒྱབ་གཉིས་ཀྱི་ཕྱིར།།
ནམ་ཡང་ཡུལ་ནས་སྡོད་པའི་དུས་མི་འབྱུང་།།
ཕྱོགས་བཅུར་འཁྱམས་ནས་ཟས་ནོར་གོས་རྣམས་བཙལ།།
གང་མགོ་ཁྱིར་ནས་འོང་བའི་དྲིན་ཅན་ཕ།།
འཇིག་རྟེན་ཕྱི་མར་སོང་བ་སྙིང་རེ་རྗེ།།
སྤྱན་རས་གཟིགས་ཀྱིས་ལམ་སྣ་དྲང་དུ་གསོལ།།
ཤུལ་ནས་བུ་ཡིས་ཅི་བྱས་དགེ་རྩ་རྣམས།།
རྗེས་སུ་འབྲངས་ནས་ཕན་ཐོགས་འབྱུང་བར་ཤོག།

Noble, Great Compassionate One, please hear my prayer.
My kind father who has cared for me with such devotion
Has gone off to his place in the next life.
Please look upon him with your unwavering gaze of compassion.
This son he left behind makes offerings to the Precious Ones,
Pays respects to the *Saṅgha*, and so on, in his name—
May all those good deeds quickly follow him,
And bring him benefit in later lives.

For the sake of his family,
He would wander in the ten directions in search of food,
    wealth, and clothing,
And never had time to stay home.
My kind father, who would return carrying "necessities" for us—
He has gone on to his next life. How sad!
I beseech you, Chenrezig, to guide him on his way.
May the virtuous deeds of his surviving son
Follow him after death and bring him benefit.

ཉིན་པར་འགྲོ་ཞིང་མཚན་མོ་ཉལ་ན་ཡང་།།
བུ་དང་བུ་མོ་མང་པོའི་ལྟོ་རྒྱབ་འདི།།
ཇི་ལྟར་བྱས་ན་རྟེན་དམ་བསམ་བློ་བཏང་།།
སེམས་ཁུར་མ་ལས་ཆེ་བའི་དྲིན་ཅན་ཕ།།
འཇིག་རྟེན་ཕྱི་མར་སོང་བ་སྙིང་རེ་རྗེ།།
སྤྱན་རས་གཟིགས་ཀྱིས་ལམ་སྣ་དྲང་དུ་གསོལ།།
ཤུལ་ནས་བུ་ཡིས་ཅི་བྱས་དགེ་རྩ་རྣམས།།
རྗེས་སུ་འབྲངས་ནས་ཕན་ཐོགས་འབྱུང་བར་ཤོག།

ཟས་ནི་ངན་ངོན་གོས་ཧྲུལ་སློག་པ་གྱོན།།
ཉིན་པར་ལྟོ་བཅག་མཚན་མོའི་གཉིད་སྐྱངས་ནས།།
ཞིང་ལས་སོ་ནམ་རེམ་པས་ཉིན་མཚན་འདས།།
ཚེ་འདིར་སྐྱིད་པོ་མ་བྱུང་དྲིན་ཅན་ཕ།།
འཇིག་རྟེན་ཕྱི་མར་སོང་བ་སྙིང་རེ་རྗེ།།
སྤྱན་རས་གཟིགས་ཀྱིས་ལམ་སྣ་དྲང་དུ་གསོལ།།
ཤུལ་ནས་བུ་ཡིས་ཅི་བྱས་དགེ་རྩ་རྣམས།།
རྗེས་སུ་འབྲངས་ནས་ཕན་ཐོགས་འབྱུང་བར་ཤོག།

Going about in the day and lying down at night,
He would always worry,
'How can I feed and clothe so many sons and daughters?'
My kind, father, even more heavy-hearted than mother—
He has gone on to his next life. How sad!
I beseech you, Chenrezig, to guide him on his way.
May the virtuous deeds of his surviving son
Follow him after death and bring him benefit.

He ate as little as he could, and wore a tattered coat.
By day he ignored hunger, and by night he gave up sleep.
Days would give way to nights as he labored in the fields.
My kind father who never knew happiness in this life—
He has gone on to his next life. How sad!
I beseech you, Chenrezig, to guide him on his way.
May the virtuous deeds of his surviving son
Follow him after death and bring him benefit.

ནོར་རྫས་བཅོལ་ནས་མ་རྙེད་རྐུ་འཕྲོག་བྱས།།
རྫུན་དང་གཡོ་སྒྱུས་ཕ་རོལ་གཞན་མགོ་བསྐོར།།
སྡིག་ལས་མང་པོ་ཞར་དང་ཞོར་ལ་བསགས།།
ཕྱི་མར་ནམ་ཡང་མི་སྐྱིད་དྲིན་ཅན་ཕ།།
འཇིག་རྟེན་ཕྱི་མར་སོང་བ་སྙིང་རེ་རྗེ།།
སྤྱན་རས་གཟིགས་ཀྱིས་ལམ་སྣ་དྲང་དུ་གསོལ།།
ཤུལ་ནས་བུ་ཡིས་ཅི་བྱས་དགེ་རྩ་རྣམས།།
རྗེས་སུ་འབྲངས་ནས་ཕན་ཐོགས་འབྱུང་བར་ཤོག།

རྒྱུན་དུ་ཚོང་དང་བུན་བསྐྱེད་འཚོ་སྐྱོང་བྱེད།།
བུ་ལ་བཟང་ཞིག་ཡོད་ན་བུ་སྐྱེས་སྙམ།།
རབ་ཏུ་དགའ་བས་ཁོང་འཛུམ་མང་པོ་བྱེད།།
ཁ་སྐྱེལ་མགོ་ལ་བྱུགས་པའི་དྲིན་ཅན་ཕ།།
འཇིག་རྟེན་ཕྱི་མར་སོང་བ་སྙིང་རེ་རྗེ།།
སྤྱན་རས་གཟིགས་ཀྱིས་ལམ་སྣ་དྲང་དུ་གསོལ།།
ཤུལ་ནས་བུ་ཡིས་ཅི་བྱས་དགེ་རྩ་རྣམས།།
རྗེས་སུ་འབྲངས་ནས་ཕན་ཐོགས་འབྱུང་བར་ཤོག།

He sought wealth and did not find it, so he stole,
And deceived others with lies and tricks.
In this way he happened to accumulate much evil karma.
My kind father who will never know happiness in later lives—
He has gone on to his next life. How sad!
I beseech you, Chenrezig, to guide him on his way.
May the virtuous deeds of his surviving son
Follow him after death and bring him benefit.

He regularly supported his family with business, and interest
from loans.
He dreamed of having a son. Oh! If only he could have
fine qualities!
After my birth, he was completely overjoyed, and always smiling.
My kind father who would kiss me and pat me on the head—
He has gone on to his next life. How sad!
I beseech you, Chenrezig, to guide him on his way.
May the virtuous deeds of his surviving son
Follow him after death and bring him benefit.

བུ་ལ་ནཚ་ཙུང་ཟད་ཙམ་བྱུང་ཡང་།།
དངངས་ནས་མོ་སྨན་རྩིས་པའི་དྲུང་དུ་རྒྱུགས།།
ཁྱིམ་ན་ཡོད་པའི་ཟས་གོས་ཕལ་ཆེ་བ།།
ཕངས་མེད་སླུད་དུ་གཏོང་བའི་དྲིན་ཅན་པ།།
འཇིག་རྟེན་ཕྱི་རོལ་སོང་བ་སྙིང་རེ་རྗེ།།
སྤྱན་རས་གཟིགས་ཀྱིས་ལམ་སྣ་དྲང་དུ་གསོལ།།
ཤུལ་ནས་བུ་ཡིས་ཅི་བྱས་དགེ་རྩ་རྣམས།།
རྗེས་སུ་འབྲངས་ནས་ཕན་ཐོགས་འབྱུང་བར་ཤོག།

བུ་དང་བུ་མོ་ཆེ་རུ་སོང་བ་ན།།
བུ་མོར་གོས་རྒྱན་བཏགས་ནས་གནས་ལ་རྫོང་།།
བུ་ནི་ལ་ལར་ཆོས་བསླབས་རབ་བྱུང་བྱས།།
ལ་ལར་ཆུང་མ་ལེན་པའི་དྲིན་ཅན་པ།།
འཇིག་རྟེན་ཕྱི་མར་སོང་བ་སྙིང་རེ་རྗེ།།
སྤྱན་རས་གཟིགས་ཀྱིས་ལམ་སྣ་དྲང་དུ་གསོལ།།
ཤུལ་ནས་བུ་ཡིས་ཅི་བྱས་དགེ་རྩ་རྣམས།།
རྗེས་སུ་འབྲངས་ནས་ཕན་ཐོགས་འབྱུང་བར་ཤོག།

When one of his children was laid low by the slightest illness,
He would run, panting, to soothsayers, doctors, and astrologers.
Whatever household goods he owned, food or clothing,
My kind father would hand over the whole lot as ransom—
He has gone on to his next life. How sad!
I beseech you, Chenrezig, to guide him on his way.
May the virtuous deeds of his surviving son
Follow him after death and bring him benefit.

When his sons and daughters got older,
He dressed up the daughters, adorned them with jewelry,
  and married them off.
Some sons he had trained in Dharma, and ordained.
Others he helped find brides. My kind father—
He has gone on to his next life. How sad!
I beseech you, Chenrezig, to guide him on his way.
May the virtuous deeds of his surviving son
Follow him after death and bring him benefit.

སྡིག་སྡུག་གཏམ་ངན་ཐམས་ཅད་ཁྲིད་དུ་བསད།།
ཤ་ཐང་བསྐྱེད་ནས་འབད་པས་བཙལ་བ་ཡི།།
ས་ཞིང་ཁང་བ་ནོར་རྫས་ཅི་ཡོད་པ།།
ཐམས་ཅད་བུ་ལ་སྤྲོད་པའི་དྲིན་ཅན་ཕ།།
འཇིག་རྟེན་ཕྱི་མར་སོང་བ་སྙིང་རེ་རྗེ།།
སྤྱན་རས་གཟིགས་ཀྱིས་ལམ་སྣ་དྲང་དུ་གསོལ།།
ཤུལ་ནས་བུ་ཡིས་ཅི་བྱས་དགེ་རྩ་རྣམས།།
རྗེས་སུ་འབྲངས་ནས་ཕན་ཐོགས་འགྱུར་བར་ཤོག།

རང་ཉིད་ལག་པ་སྟོང་བར་གྱུར་ན་ཡང་།།
བདག་གིས་ཐམས་ཅད་བུ་ལ་འཕྲོད་དོ་ཟེར།།
ད་ནི་འཕྲོད་སར་འཕྲོད་ནི་ཡིན་ནོ་ཞེས།།
སླར་ཡང་དགའ་དགའ་བྱེད་པའི་དྲིན་ཅན་ཕ།།
འཇིག་རྟེན་ཕྱི་མར་སོང་བ་སྙིང་རེ་རྗེ།།
སྤྱན་རས་གཟིགས་ཀྱིས་ལམ་སྣ་དྲང་དུ་གསོལ།།
ཤུལ་ནས་བུ་ཡིས་ཅི་བྱས་དགེ་རྩ་རྣམས།།
རྗེས་སུ་འབྲངས་ནས་ཕན་ཐོགས་འགྱུར་བར་ཤོག།

Though performing evil deeds and suffering, he ignored
    the spiteful gossip of others.
My kind father, who bequeathed to his sons
Whatever he amassed through great hardship and exhaustion—
Land, house, and wealth—
He has gone on to his next life. How sad!
I beseech you, Chenrezig, to guide him on his way.
May the virtuous deeds of his surviving son
Follow him after death and bring him benefit.

"Although my own hands will be left empty,
I bequeath everything to my sons," he said.
"I am now giving everything to my rightful heirs,"
    he declared again and again.
My kind father, who could not contain his joy at this thought—
He has gone on to his next life. How sad!
I beseech you, Chenrezig, to guide him on his way.
May the virtuous deeds of his surviving son
Follow him after death and bring him benefit.

དེ་ལྟར་ཚེ་འདིར་བསྒྲུངས་པའི་དྲིན་ཆེན་ཕས།།
དོན་མེད་བཟའ་ཚང་ལྟོ་རྒྱབ་བསྒྲུབས་བསྒྲུབས་ནས།།
དོན་ཆེན་དམ་ཆོས་བསྒྲུབ་པའི་ལོམ་མ་བྱུང་།།
ཚེ་འདིར་བསྒྲུངས་པའི་བུ་དང་བུ་མོ་བྲལ།།
འཇིག་རྟེན་ཕྱི་མར་སོང་བ་སྙིང་རེ་རྗེ།།
སྤྱན་རས་གཟིགས་ཀྱིས་ལམ་སྣ་དྲང་དུ་གསོལ།།
ཤུལ་ནས་བུ་ཡིས་ཅི་བྱས་དགེ་རྩ་རྣམས།།
རྗེས་སུ་འབྲངས་ནས་ཕན་ཐོགས་འགྱུར་བར་ཤོག།

ཅེས་པ་དྲིན་ཅན་གྱི་ཕ་ཤི་བའི་དགེ་རྩའི་སྟེང་ནས་བསྐུལ་ཚིག་པ་འདི་ཡང་ཚོགས་དྲུག་རང་གྲོལ་གྱིས་སྨྲས་པའོ།།

My kind father who supported us in this life
By acquiring useless food and clothes for his family over and over—
Never had free time to practice what is meaningful,
    the holy Dharma.
Now he is deprived of those very sons and daughters for whom
    he sacrificed.
He has gone on to his next life. How sad!
I beseech you, Chenrezig, to guide him on his way.
May the virtuous deeds of his surviving son
Follow him after death and bring him benefit.

I, Tshogdruk Rangdrol, dedicated the roots of the virtue I had performed to my kind father at the time of his death, and also spoke this invocation to Chenrezig.

Chapter Four

Nature

དགུང་སྔོན་མཐོན་པོ་ལ་བྱ་རྒོད་ལྡིང་བ་བཞིན།།
མཐའ་བྲལ་ཆོས་དབྱིངས་ཀྱི་ནམ་མཁའ་ཡངས་པ་ལ།།
རང་རིག་འཛིན་མེད་ཀྱི་བྱ་རྒོད་འཕྱོ་ན་ཨང་།།

བར་སྣང་ཡངས་པ་ན་སྤྲིན་དཀར་འཕྱུར་བ་བཞིན།།
དབྱིངས་རིག་དབྱེར་མེད་ཀྱི་བར་སྣང་ཡངས་པ་ལ།།
བདེ་གསལ་མི་རྟོག་པའི་སྤྲིན་དཀར་ལངས་ན་ཨང་།།

འོད་སྟོང་ཕྱོགས་བཅུ་རུ་སྒྲོ་བའི་ཉི་མ་བཞིན།།
མཐའ་མེད་འགྲོ་ཀུན་གྱི་པདྨོའི་སྐྱེད་ཚལ་དུ།།
འགག་མེད་སྙིང་རྗེ་ཡི་ཉི་མ་ཤར་ན་ཨང་།།

སྐྱི་བསེར་རླུང་པོ་ཕོ་ཕྱོགས་ཀུན་འཕྱོ་བ་བཞིན།།
གཞན་ཕན་འཕྲིན་ལས་ཀྱི་ཤུགས་འབྱུང་སྐྱི་བསེར་རླུང་།།
ཕྱོགས་རིས་ཐོགས་རྡུགས་མེད་ཀུན་ལ་འཕྱོ་ན་ཨང་།།

ལྷོ་ཕྱོགས་ནམ་མཁའ་ན་འབྲུག་ཅིག་ལྡིར་བ་བཞིན།།
སྐལ་བཟང་གདུལ་བྱ་ཡི་མདངས་ལྡན་དགའ་སྟོན་དུ།།
ཟབ་རྒྱས་ལེགས་བཤད་ཀྱི་དབྲུར་ཟ་ལྡིར་ན་ཨང་།།

Like an eagle that soars in the lofty blue heights,
The eagle of my nongrasping awareness
Flies in the broad space of the limitless *dharmadhātu*. Hey!

Like white clouds rising up in wide open sky,
White clouds of bliss, clarity, and non-thought
Rise up in the wide open sky of indivisible space and awareness. Hey!

Like the sun, whose brilliance radiates out in the ten directions,
The sun of limitless compassion
Shines upon the lotus grove of countless sentient beings. Hey!

Like the winds rushing forth in all directions,
The spontaneously arising wind of beneficial actions
Rushes forth indiscriminately in all directions. Hey!

Like the thunder-dragon that roars in the southern sky,
Summer drums that eloquently expound the profound and
vast Dharma
Roar at the feast of peacocks fortunate enough to be tamed. Hey!

ཟིམ་བུའི་སྦྲང་ཆར་ཞིག་དལ་བུས་འབབ་པ་བཞིན།།
དང་ལྡན་ཞིང་ས་རུ་བྱིན་རླབས་ཆར་བབས་ནས།།
ཉམས་རྟོགས་ཡོན་ཏན་གྱི་མྱུ་གུ་འཁྲུངས་ན་ཨང་།།

ཞེས་པ་འདི་ཡང་ཉིན་ཞིག་ནམ་མཁའ་མཐོན་པོའི་དབྱིངས་རུམ་ན་བྱ་རྒོད་ཅིག་ལྡིང་ཞིང་། ཕྱོགས་ཕྱོགས་ཀྱི་རི་རྩེའི་བར་སྣང་ལ་སྤྲིན་དཀར་གྱེན་དུ་འཕྱུར། ལྷོ་ཕྱོགས་ན་གཡུ་འབྲུག་ཅིག་ལྡིར་ཞིང་སྦྲང་ཆར་འབབ་པ། སྐྱི་སེར་རླུང་འཇམ་པོ་དལ་བུར་རྒྱུ་བ་སོགས་ཀྱིས་རྒྱན་བྱས་ཡོད་ལ་འདི་ཤར་ཚོ་འཕྲལ་དུ་ཡི་གེར་བྲིས་པའོ།།

Like the fine, pleasant rains that gently fall,

Rains of blessings fall on the fields of the faithful,

And reeds of experience, realization, and qualities sprout up. Hey!

This gur came to mind one day when I saw an eagle soaring in the womb of the space of the high sky, white clouds rising up in the atmosphere around surrounding mountain peaks, a turquoise thunder-dragon roaring in the south, a pleasant rain falling, a soft wind gently stirring, and so forth. At that time, I immediately put it down in writing.

ལྡོན་ཤིང་ཡལ་ག་ཁྱོད་ད་ལྟ་འགུལ་སྐྱོད་འདྲ་མ་མང་།།
བྱ་རྒྱལ་ཁུ་བྱུག་ང་ཡང་ཡང་ཁྱོད་སྟེང་ནས་མི་གྲག།
སྟོན་གསུམ་ནམ་ཟླ་པོ་སླེབས་དུས་མྱུར་དུ་རང་འགྲོ་ངེས།།

མདངས་ལྡན་མེ་ཏོག་ཁྱོད་ད་ལྟ་འགུལ་འཁྲུག་འདྲ་མ་མང་།།
ཡིད་འོང་བུང་བ་ང་ཡང་ཡང་ཁྱོད་སྟེང་ལ་མི་འབབ།།
ཟམ་ཟིམ་ཁ་ཆར་པོ་སླེབས་ན་མྱུར་དུ་རང་འགྲོ་ངེས།།

དམ་ལྡན་མཆེད་གྲོགས་རྣམས་ད་ལྟ་ཙ་ཙོ་རང་མ་མང་།།
སྐལ་ལྡན་བྱ་བཏང་ང་ས་འདིར་ཡང་ཡང་ནི་མི་འོང་།།
སྐྱོ་ཤས་ཤུགས་དྲག་པོ་སྐྱེས་ན་མྱུར་དུ་རང་འགྲོ་ངེས།།

ཞེས་པ་འདི་ཡང་མཆེད་གྲོགས་མང་པོས་ཚེ་བློས་བཏང་སྟེ་ཡུལ་ཕྱོགས་གཞན་དུ་འགྲོ་མི་ཐུབ་ཟེར་བ་ཐོས་པའི་ལན་དུ་བྲིས་པའོ།།

Tree branches—you are shaking and moving around so much!
I, a cuckoo, king of birds, will not sit on you and sing out again
and again.
When the three months of autumn arrive, I will surely be off quickly.

Lustrous flowers—you are shaking and stirring about so much!
I, an attractive bee, will not land on you again and again.
When the light rains and snows arrive, I will surely be off quickly.

Holy, spiritual friends—you are now making such a racket
pounding flour in that watermill!
I, a fortunate renunciant, will not come here again and again.
When my disillusion with the world grows fiercer, I will surely
be off quickly.

I wrote this in reply to my spiritual friends, when I heard many of them say that if they went to another place, they would not be able to renounce concerns for this life.

གནས་ཡིད་འོང་མཚོ་སྙིང་ཁོར་ཡུག་གི།།
ཤིང་སྡོ་ལྗང་མེ་ཏོག་འདབ་རྒྱས་ཚེ།།
ཕ་བླ་མའི་སྐུ་མཛེས་ཡང་ཡང་དྲན།།

ཡིད་བག་ཕེབས་ཆུ་བྱ་སྣ་ཚོགས་ཀྱིས།།
སྐད་སྙན་མོ་དར་དིར་སྒྲོག་པའི་ཚེ།།
ཕ་བླ་མའི་གསུང་སྙན་ཡང་ཡང་དྲན།།

སྙིང་མཐོ་ལ་ཡངས་པའི་ནམ་མཁའ་ལ།།
སྤྲིན་མེད་པར་ས་ལེར་འདུག་པའི་ཚེ།།
ཕ་བླ་མའི་ཐུགས་དགོངས་ཡིད་ལ་དྲན།།

ཆུ་དྭངས་བསིལ་རྙོག་མེད་མཚོ་སྔོན་ལ།།
རླབས་ཆུ་གཉེར་རི་མོ་གཡོ་བའི་ཚེ།།
ཕ་བླ་མའི་ཡོན་ཏན་ཡང་ཡང་དྲན།།

ཤར་རི་བོའི་རྩེ་ནས་ནམ་མཁའ་ལ།།
འོད་ལམ་ལམ་ཉིམ་ཤར་བའི་ཚེ།།
ཕ་བླ་མའི་འཕྲིན་ལས་ཡང་ཡང་དྲན།།

When flowers on the lush trees
Blossom all around the lovely island, Tshonying,
I recall again and again the beautiful bodily form of father, lama.

When flocks of carefree waterbirds
Call out with delightful, quavering voices,
I recall again and again the pleasing speech of father, lama.

When the sky is cloudlessly clear and vivid
And wide open to its heights,
I recall again and again the wisdom mind of father, lama.

When patterns of waves and ripples
Ruffle the surface of cool, clear Lake Kokonor,
I recall again and again the qualities of father, lama.

When the sun rises into the sky with dazzling splendor
From behind the peak of an eastern mountain,
I recall again and again the enlightened deeds of father, lama.

ཕ་དྲིན་ཆེན་བླ་མ་རིན་པོ་ཆེ།།
ཞིང་དག་པ་རབ་འབྱམས་གར་བཞུགས་ཀྱང་།།
བུར་ཡེ་ཤེས་སྤྱན་གྱིས་རྒྱང་ནས་གཟིགས།།

ཞེས་པ་འདི་ཡང་ཉིན་གཅིག་ཕ་བླ་མ་ཆོས་རྒྱལ་དག་གི་དབང་པོ་དྲན་པའི་ཤུགས་ཀྱིས་སྨྲས་པའོ།།

O father, precious lama of infinite kindness,

Wherever you reside within the innumerable Pure Realms,

Please look upon your son from afar, with eyes of wisdom.

I said this one day, moved by memories of my father, lama Chögyäl Ngakyi Wangpo.

དགེ་སྦྱོར་གྱི་པདྨར།།
དད་གུས་ཆུ་བླུགས་ཆེ།།
ཁ་ཏོན་གྱི་འདབ་མ།།
རྗེ་རྒྱས་སུ་བུད་ཐལ།།
རྣམ་གཡེང་གི་སེར་བས།།
མ་བརྡུངས་པ་བཟང་ཡ།།

འདོད་ཆུང་གི་བྲག་རི།།
ཆོག་ཤེས་སྤྱང་བརྒྱན་ཆེ།།
དགའ་བདེ་ཡི་རྩེ་ཤིང་།།
སྣ་ཚོགས་པ་སྐྱེས་ཐལ།།
མངོན་ཞེན་གྱི་ཐོག་གིས།།
མ་བཤིག་པ་བཟང་ཡ།།

སྐྱོ་ཤས་ཀྱི་འཇོལ་མོ།།
སྐྱོ་མགུར་འདྲོགས་ཕུད་ཆེ།།
རི་ཁྲོད་ཀྱི་ཤིང་ཁར།།
ཡར་ཡར་དུ་འཕུར་ཐལ།།
འདོད་ཡོན་གྱི་ཁྲ་ཡིས།།
མ་བཟུང་བ་བཟང་ཡ།།

When the water of faith and respect
Was poured on the lotuses of virtuous practice,
Petals of chanting came fully into bloom.
That the hail of distraction
Did not strike them is good. Hey!

When the rock mountain of few desires,
Was adorned by the meadow of contentment,
Fruit trees of joy and happiness sprang up.
That the lightning of grasping at things as real
Did not destroy them is good. Hey!

When the thrush of disillusion with the world
Burst forth with a startlingly melancholy song,
It flew up and up to the top of a tree
On a secluded mountain.
That the hawk of sensory enjoyments
Did not seize it is good. Hey!

ཚུལ་ཁྲིམས་ཀྱི་བུ་མོ།།
ཞི་དུལ་རྒྱན་སྤྲས་ཆེ།།
ལེགས་སྤྱོད་ཀྱི་གནས་ལ།།
དགའ་བཞིན་དུ་བཞུད་ཐལ།།
ལོག་སྤྱོད་ཀྱི་ཨ་ནེས།།
མ་མནར་བ་བཟང་ཡ།།

བསམ་གཏན་གྱི་ཤ་བ།།
དྲན་ཤེས་རྩྭས་འགྲངས་ཆེ།།
བདེ་གསལ་མི་རྟོག་པའི།།
སྤང་ག་ཤོངས་སུ་ཉལ་ཐལ།།
བྲིང་རྐོད་ཀྱི་ཤ་ཁྲིས།།
མ་བཟུང་བ་བཟང་ཡ།།

ཤེས་རབ་ཀྱི་མར་མེ།།
ཆེས་ཆེར་དུ་སྦར་ཆེ།།
བླང་དོར་གྱི་གནས་རྣམས།།
ཙུང་ཟད་ཙིག་མཐོང་ཐལ།།
མི་ཤེས་ཀྱི་མུན་པས།།
མ་ཁེབས་པ་བཟང་ཡ།།

ཞེས་པ་འདི་ཡང་གླུ་བ་ཚོགས་དྲུག་རང་གྲོལ་གྱིས་ཉམས་དགའ་བའི་ཤུགས་ཀྱིས་བླངས་པའོ།།

When the daughter of moral discipline
Was adorned with ornaments of peace and temperance,
She went off joyfully
To a place of righteous activity.
That her paternal aunt of wrongdoing
Did not torment her is good. Hey!

When the deer of meditative concentration
Had sated itself on the grass of mindfulness and understanding,
He lay down in the grassy meadow
Of bliss, clarity, and non-thought.
That the hunting dog of torpor and agitation
Did not seize him is good. Hey!

When the butter lamp of wisdom
Blazed brighter and brighter,
What to accept and what to reject
Could be discerned a bit more clearly.
That the darkness of not-knowing
Did not conceal this is good. Hey!

The singer Tshogdruk Rangdrol also sang this, moved by delight.

Chapter Five

Death

སྐྱབས་གནས་ཐམས་ཅད་འདུས་པའི་སྐུ།།
མཚན་ལྡན་བླ་མ་རིན་པོ་ཆེ།།
གསོལ་བ་འདེབས་སོ་བདག་གཞན་གྱི།།
ཤེས་རྒྱུད་བྱིན་གྱིས་བརླབ་ཏུ་གསོལ།།

ཚེ་འདིའི་དོན་གཉེར་བློ་ལོག་ནས།།
ཆོས་ལ་བློ་ཁ་ཕྱོགས་པའི་ཕྱིར།།
མི་རྟག་འཆི་བ་དྲན་པར་བྱ།།

འཆི་བ་མ་དྲན་ཚེ་འདིར་ཆགས།།
དམ་ཆོས་ཡིད་ལ་མི་འོང་བས།།
འཆི་བ་དྲན་པ་གལ་རེ་ཆེ།།
སྐབས་སྐབས་འདི་ལྟར་དྲན་པར་བྱ།།

རང་གི་ཕ་མ་བླ་མ་དང་།།
གྲོགས་མཆེད་ཡོན་བདག་ཕོ་མོ་དང་།།
སྡེ་བ་ཚོ་བ་ཡུལ་ཕྱོགས་ཀྱི།།
མི་རྣམས་མང་པོ་ཤི་བ་བགྲངས།།
རང་ཡང་འདི་ཡི་རང་བཞིན་ཡིན།།

I pray to the precious, qualified lama,
Embodiment which subsumes all sources of refuge.
Please bless my mind-stream
And that of others.

I will now give advice to all who hear this song.
After turning against the pursuit of concerns for this life,
You should call to mind transitory death,
In order to turn your sentiments towards the Dharma.

If you don't reflect upon death, you will cling to this life,
And will not be involved with the holy Dharma,
So the importance of recollecting death is great.
Sometimes you should recall it like this:

Count how many people have died
Even in your homeland—
Your own father and mother, lamas,
Friends, siblings, and male and female patrons—
It's the same for you.

སྤྱོད་རྩིས་བྱས་པས་ཅི་ཞིག་བྱ།།
ཕྱི་མར་འགྲོ་བའི་གྲབས་ཞོམ་བྱ།།
སྙམ་དུ་ཕྱུག་སྐོར་ཁ་ཧྲོན་གྱིས།།
རང་དང་ལོ་མཉམ་ཤི་བ་དང་།།
རང་གི་ཆུང་རྣམས་ཤི་བ་སོམས།།
རང་ཡང་འདི་ཡི་རང་བཞིན་ཡིན།།

ད་སྔ་མ་ཤི་ཡ་མཚན་ཆེ།།
མ་ཤི་ན་ཡང་ཚེ་འདི་ཡི།།
རྣམ་གཡེང་འདུ་འཛིའི་དབང་སོང་ནས།།
འཇིག་རྟེན་ཕྱི་མར་སོང་བའི་ཚེ།།
ཕན་པའི་དམ་ཆོས་མ་བྱས་ན།།
སྐྱོན་ཆེ་ཆོས་ལ་འབད་པར་བྱ།།
སྙམ་དུ་བླ་མ་དཀོན་མཆོག་མཆོད།།
དབུལ་ཕོངས་རྣམས་ལ་སྦྱིན་པ་ཐོངས།།

གཞན་ཡང་སྒོ་ཕྱུགས་ཤི་བ་དང་།།
བྱ་དང་རི་དྭགས་འབུ་སྲིན་སོགས།།
ཤི་བ་མཐོང་དང་ཐོས་ན་ཡང་།།
རང་ཡང་འདི་ཡི་རང་བཞིན་ཡིན།།

What good will it do to count on living?
You should prepare and make plans for going on to
  your next life—
With this in mind, perform prostrations, circumambulations,
  and chants.
Think about the deaths of those your own age,
And the deaths of those younger than you.
It's the same for you.

It's amazing that you haven't died already.
Even though you haven't died,
If you are influenced by distractions and clamor in this life,
And do not practice the rewarding, holy Dharma,
When you go on to your next life the penalty will be great.
You should exert yourself in spiritual practice
With this in mind, make offerings to your lama and
  the Precious Ones
And give gifts to the poor.

Furthermore, when you see or hear about the deaths
Of domestic cattle
And the deaths of birds, deer, insects, and so on—
It's the same for you.

ཚེ་འདིར་ཆགས་པས་ཅི་ཞིག་བྱ།།
ཕྱི་མར་སྐྱིད་པའི་ཆོས་ཤིག་དགོས།།
སྙམ་དུ་ཚོགས་གསོག་སྒྲིབ་སྦྱོང་གྱིས།།

གཞན་ཡང་ཤི་བའི་རོ་རྣུས་པ།།
ལ་སོགས་མཐོང་དུས་འདི་སྐྱེས་ནས།།
ཤི་བ་ཡིན་པས་རང་ཉིད་ཀྱང་།།
ནམ་ཞིག་འདི་ཡི་རང་བཞིན་ཡིན།།

གཉིད་དང་བཟའ་བཏུང་དབང་སོང་ནས།།
ཆོས་མེད་ལག་སྟོང་འགྲོ་ཉེན་འདུག།
ཕྱི་མར་བདེ་བའི་ཆོས་བྱ་དགོས།།
སྙམ་དུ་ཐོས་བསམ་སྒོམ་གསུམ་གྱིས།།

འདི་ཡང་ཚོགས་དྲུག་རང་གྲོལ་གླངས།།
དགེ་འདིས་རང་གཞན་མ་ལུས་པ།།
གནས་སྐབས་ཀུན་ཏུ་བདེ་བ་དང་།།
མཐར་ཐུག་རྣམ་མཁྱེན་མྱུར་ཐོབ་ཤོག།

What good will it do to cling to this life?
You need the Dharma for happiness in your next life.
With this in mind, gather the two accumulations and purify
your obscurations.

Furthermore, when you see
Corpses, bones of the dead, and so on—
You should realize that these beings were also born, and later died.
Even you, eventually, will die—
It's the same for you.

Influenced by sleep, food, and drink,
There is the danger of departing empty-handed, without religion.
With this in mind, you must practice the Dharma for the happiness
of future lives—
Listen to, reflect upon, and meditate on the holy teachings.

Tshogdruk Rangdrol sang this song.
Through this merit, may myself and others, without exception,
Find temporary happiness,
And may we quickly attain ultimate omniscience.

དང་པོ་བླ་མའི་དྲུང་ནས་ཐོས་བསམ་བྱས།།
བར་དུ་རི་ཁྲོད་དབེན་པར་གཅིག་པར་བསྒོམས།།
ཐ་མར་བསྟན་དང་འགྲོ་ལ་གང་ཕན་བྱས།།
མི་རྒན་ང་ཡི་བྱ་བ་ཚར་ནས་གདའ།།

ད་ནི་ཚེ་མཇུག་ལ་མགོའི་ཉི་ཟེར་ཙམ།།
ཡུན་ཐུང་ནམ་འཆི་ཆ་ཡང་མི་འདུག་པས།།
གཞོན་པའི་དུས་བཞིན་འགྲོ་འདུག་མི་མང་བར།།
དབེན་པར་སྐྱིད་ཉལ་རྒྱག་པའི་དུས་ལ་བབས།།

དམ་པ་གོང་མའི་བྱིན་གྱིས་བརླབས་པའི་གནས།།
ས་ཆུ་འཁྲོད་ཅིང་མཐུན་རྐྱེན་འཛོམས་པ་ཡི།།
རི་ཁྲོད་ཉམས་དགའ་ཞིག་ཏུ་འཆི་ནུས་ན།།
རྣལ་འབྱོར་བདག་གི་བསམ་པ་རྫོགས་པ་ཡིན།།

ཚེ་འདིར་རི་ཁྲོད་གང་དུ་ཕྱིན་ན་ཡང་།།
སྒྲུབ་ལ་བར་ཆད་མེད་པ་བླ་མའི་དྲིན།།
དྲིན་ལན་སྒྲུབ་པའི་མཆོད་པ་རྒྱུན་དུ་འབུལ།།
སྒྲུབ་ལ་བར་ཆད་མེད་པར་བྱིན་གྱིས་རློབས།།

In the beginning, I listened to and contemplated the Dharma
in the presence of a lama.
Later, I meditated alone in a mountain hermitage.
Finally, I created whatever benefit I could for the teachings
and sentient beings.
Now I am an old man, and my activities are finished.

Here at the end of life, a mere glimmer of sunlight on a mountain peak,
It is uncertain how soon I will die,
But the time has come to lay my body down happily in a solitary place,
Without bustling about as in youth.

If I am able to die in a delightful hermitage,
A place blessed by the holy ones of former times,
Where the land and water are suitable and favorable circumstances
come together,
My intentions, as a yogi, will be fulfilled.

Whenever I arrive at a mountain hermitage,
I always offer up my practices to repay
The kindness of lamas, which removes impediments to practice.
Please bless me, so there will be no obstacles.

གངས་རྫ་གཡའ་དང་ནགས་ཚལ་དུར་ཁྲོད་སོགས།།
ཡིད་མཐུན་བག་ཕེབས་རི་ཡི་རྒྱུད་བཟང་ཞིང་།།
བྱིན་ལྡན་མ་མོ་མཁའ་འགྲོ་འདུ་བའི་ས།།
དུས་ཀུན་རྒྱུན་དུ་བསྟེན་པའི་བཀྲ་ཤིས་ཤོག།

ཅེས་པ་འདི་ནི་ཆོས་བྱེད་པོའི་དང་ལ་མི་ཚེ་ཤོར་བའི་རྣལ་འབྱོར་ཞབས་དཀར་བས་རང་ལོ་དྲུག་ཅུ་རྩ་དྲུག་ཐོག་ཏུ་སླེབས་ཚེ། ཉིན་ཞིག་སེམས་ལ་ཤར་བ་ལྟར་དབེན་གནས་བཀྲ་ཤིས་འཁྱིལ་བ་ནས་སྨྲས་པའོ།།

May good fortune come to those who continually stay
In such places as snow-covered mountains, clay mountains,
slate mountains,
Forests, groves, cemeteries, good, agreeable, restful mountain ranges,
And places where *mamo*s and *ḍākinī*s gather and give blessings.

I who am practicing the Dharma in old age, the yogi Shabkar from whom a human life has been slipping away, said this one day when I reached the age of sixty-six at the hermitage Tashikhyil, in accordance with what came to mind.

དམར་སེར་མེ་ཏོག་པད་ཚལ།།
བ་མོས་བཅོམ་ན་མི་རུང་།།
བསམས་ནས་ལོ་འདབ་བཞད་དུས།།
སྦྲང་རྩི་མང་བོ་བསྡུས་སོང་།།
ད་ནི་བ་མོ་བྱུང་ཡང་།།
བུང་བ་འགྱོད་པ་མི་སྣང་།།

ཞིང་བཟང་ལོ་ཡག་སྙི་མ།།
སེར་བ་ཐོག་ན་མི་རུང་།།
བསམས་ནས་འབྲས་བུ་སྨིན་དུས།།
སྟོན་ཐོག་ཁྱིམ་དུ་བསྡུས་སོང་།།
ད་ནི་སེར་བ་བྱུང་ཡང་།།
ཞིང་བདག་འགྱོད་པ་མི་སྣང་།།

ཡང་ཡང་ཐོབ་དཀའི་མི་ལུས།།
འཆི་ནད་བྱུང་ན་མི་རུང་།།
བསམས་ནས་ལུས་སེམས་བདེ་དུས།།
ཉམས་ལེན་རྒྱུད་ལ་སྦྱར་སོང་།།
ད་ནི་འཆི་བ་བྱུང་ཡང་།།
རྣལ་འབྱོར་འགྱོད་པ་མི་སྣང་།།

'The grove of crimson lotuses
Must not be injured by frost.'
Thinking about that, when the lotuses blossomed,
The bees gathered lots of nectar.
Now, although the frost has arrived,
The bees have no regrets.

'The ears of grain in an excellent field in a good year
Must not be struck by hail.'
Remembering that, when the seeds matured,
The farmer gathered the harvest into the house.
Now although the hail has arrived,
The field-owner has no regrets.

'A human body, difficult to attain again and again,
Must not be overcome by illness and death.'
Realizing that, while the yogi's body and mind were still healthy,
He joined practice with his mind-stream.
Now although the point of death has arrived,
The yogi has no regrets.

སེང་གེ་དཀར་མོའི་ཕྲུ་གུ་དེ།།
ཨ་མའི་མངལ་ནས་རྩལ་གསུམ་རྫོགས།།
མངལ་གྱི་རྒྱུ་ལས་གྲོལ་བ་དང་།།
གདངས་དཀར་སྟོད་དུ་འཕྱོ་བར་ངེས།།

བྱ་རྒྱལ་ཁྱུང་གི་ཕྲུ་གུ་དེ།།
སྒོ་ངའི་ནང་ནས་གཤོག་སྒྲོ་རྒྱས།།
སྒོ་ངའི་རྒྱུ་ལས་གྲོལ་བ་དང་།།
དགུང་སྔོན་མཁའ་ལ་འཕྱུར་བར་ངེས།།

རྣལ་འབྱོར་པ་ཡི་སེམས་ཉིད་དེ།།
ལུས་ཀྱི་ནང་ནས་ཉམས་རྟོགས་རྒྱས།།
ལུས་ཀྱི་རྒྱུ་ལས་གྲོལ་བ་དང་།།
འཆི་བ་ཆོས་སྐུར་གྲོལ་བར་ངེས།།

ཞེས་བླངས་པས་ཀུན་དད་ཅིང་གུས་པར་གྱུར་ཏོ།།

The cub of the white lion
Has perfected the three skills in its mother's womb.
It will surely be freed from the enclosure of the womb
And roam the peaks of the snow-covered mountains.

The chick of the *garuḍa*, king of birds,
Has developed feathers and wings within the egg.
It will certainly be freed from the enclosure of the egg
And fly about in the blue sky.

The unborn mind of the yogi
Has developed profound experiences and realization within the body.
It will definitely be freed from the enclosure of the body
And be liberated into the *dharmakāya* at death.

When I sang this, everyone gained faith and respect.

Chapter Six

Renunciation

ནོར་ནི་དང་པོ་བདག་སྐྱིད་པོ།
བསོད་ནམས་ཅན་ཟེར་གཞན་སྨོན་པོ།
ཡོད་ཀྱིན་ད་དུང་ཡོད་ན་སྙམ།
ཅི་ཙམ་ཡོད་ཀྱང་ཚོག་ཤེས་མེད།།

བར་དུ་ཕྱུགས་ལུག་བཏང་འདོགས་ཀྱིས།
ཆར་ཆུའི་ནང་ན་འོ་རེ་བརྒྱལ།
ཕྱུགས་རྣམས་རི་ཁར་བཏང་ནས་བཟུང་།།
རྐུན་ཧག་ཨ་འོང་ཨ་འོང་སྙམ།
སྤྲང་གིས་ཕྱུགས་རྣམས་གསོད་ཀྱིས་དོགས།

བཀྲེས་སྐོམ་ལྟོང་བཞིན་ལེགས་ཉེས་བལྟས།
སྡོད་ནས་རྐུན་མ་བྱུང་གིས་དོགས།
མཚན་མོའི་གཉིད་ཀྱི་བདེ་བ་བཀག
དགེ་བའི་ཕྱོགས་སུ་གཏོང་མི་ཕོད།།
དམ་ཆོས་འོང་བའི་གོ་སྐབས་མེད།།

ཕལ་ཆེར་རང་ཡང་མྱུ་གེས་འཆི།།
སྡུག་བསྔལ་དྲག་པོས་སེམས་རྗུ་ནོན།།
སྐབས་སྐབས་ཧག་པ་རྐུན་མས་འཁྱེར།།
ར་མདར་བརྒྱུགས་ནས་རང་ཡང་གསོད།།

At first, wealth was my happiness.
To have merit was the prayer of others.
Whenever I had expensive things, I would wonder where they were.
Whatever I had was still not enough.

Later on, I would take cattle and sheep out to pasture and bring them back at night.
One day they got caught in a flash flood, and were exhausted.
I herded them onto the flank of the mountain, and rounded them up.
'Would a robber come, would he?,' I agonized.
'Would a wolf kill the cattle?' I wondered.

Hungry and thirsty, I looked at the *Legnye*.
After dark, I was so frightened a thief would show up
I could hardly sleep that night.
I couldn't turn my thoughts towards virtue,
And there was no chance for the holy Dharma to come to me.

I thought I would probably die of hunger,
And fierce suffering shook me to the roots:
'Thieves sometimes steal cattle and sheep,
And if I chased after them, they might even kill me.'

འཁྲུང་སྣ་འདྲེན་པའི་རྒྱུ་ནོར་དེ།།
དགྲ་འདྲེ་འབོད་པའི་གཡབ་མོ་འདྲ།།

ཐ་མར་སྦྲང་མའི་སྦྲང་རྩི་བཞིན།།
རང་གིས་སྤྱད་པར་མ་ཐོད་པའི།།
ནོར་རྣམས་གཞན་གྱིས་ཅི་བདེར་སྤྱོད།།
རང་ཉིད་ཕྱི་མར་ལག་སྟོང་འགྲོ།།

དེ་ཕྱིར་ཚོགས་དྲུག་རང་གྲོལ་ཁྱོད།།
རྒྱུ་ནོར་འཛོམས་པའི་གནས་སྐབས་སུ།།
བསགས་པའི་ནོར་ལ་སྙིང་པོ་ལོངས།།
གང་ཡོད་ཆོས་ཀྱི་ཕྱོགས་སུ་ཐོངས།།

མ་གསོགས་མ་གསོགས་ནོར་མ་གསོགས།།
བསོག་ན་འཕགས་པའི་ནོར་བདུན་གསོགས།།

ཞེས་པ་འདི་ཡང་ཚོགས་དྲུག་རང་གྲོལ་གྱིས་རང་ལ་སླབ་པའོ།།

Riches, which invite one's downfall,
Are like hand signals beckoning enemies and ghosts.

Now I feel that wealth is like nectar on the edge of a sword
luring a bee,
And I dare not be involved with it.
Though others can do as they please,
From now on I'll go empty-handed.

Therefore, you, Tshogdruk Rangdrol,
Take advantage of the wealth you have.
Whenever you have plenty of resources,
Give them all to the Dharma.

Don't accumulate, don't accumulate. Don't accumulate wealth.
If you do accumulate something, make sure it is the seven riches.

I, Tshogdruk Rangdrol, said this to myself.

བོད་ཡུལ་གངས་རི་ལྷ་བུ་ན།།
སྒྲིབ་མེད་སེང་གེ་འཁྱོ་འདྲ་བའི།།
རྗེ་བཙུན་མི་ལ་རས་པ་ལ།།
གསོལ་བ་འདེབས་སོ་བྱིན་གྱིས་རློབས།།

ལྷོ་གོས་ཚེ་འདི་བློས་བཏང་ནས།།
གངས་རྫ་གཡའ་དང་ནགས་ཚལ་སོགས།།
དབེན་པའི་གནས་སུ་གཅིག་པུ་རུ།།
དམ་ཆོས་ཉམས་སུ་ལེན་པའི་ཚེ།།
རེ་འགའ་གོས་བཟང་གྱོན་ན་འདོད།།
གོས་བཟང་གྱོན་ན་འདོད་པའི་ཚེ།།
གོས་སུ་ངན་ངོན་དུག་རྩུལ་གྱོན།།
འཇམ་ལེགས་སྒྲུ་མ་ལྷ་བུར་ལྷོས།།

རེས་འགའ་ཟས་ཞིམ་ཟོས་ན་འདོད།།
ཟས་ཞིམ་ཟོས་ན་འདོད་པའི་ཚེ།།
ངན་ངོན་ཙམ་གྱིས་ཆོག་ཤེས་ཀྱིས།།
ཞིམ་མངར་སྒྲུ་མ་ལྷ་བུར་ལྷོས།།

I pray to the lord Milarepa,
Who roamed the glacial mountains of Tibet
Like an unbridled lion.
Please bless me.

I renounced food, clothing, and other concerns for this life.
But when I practice the holy Dharma
Alone in solitary places—
Glaciers, clay or slate mountains, forests—
Sometimes I long to wear fine clothing.
And when I long to do so,
I should put on the worst rags
And see softness and quality as illusions.

Sometimes I crave delicious food,
And when I crave such food,
I should be happy to eat a few scraps,
And see delicious and sweet things as illusions.

རེས་འགའ་ནོར་རྫས་གསོག་ན་འདོད།།
ནོར་རྫས་གསོག་ན་འདོད་པའི་ཚེ།།
ནོར་ནི་འཕགས་པའི་ནོར་བདུན་གསོགས།།
ནོར་རྫས་སྒྱུ་མ་ལྟ་བུར་ལྟོས།།

རེས་འགའ་ཡུལ་དུ་སོང་ན་འདོད།།
ཡུལ་དུ་སོང་ན་འདོད་པའི་ཚེ།།
ཡུལ་ནི་ཆོས་དབྱིངས་ཕོ་བྲང་ཟུངས།།
ཕ་ཡུལ་སྒྱུ་མ་ལྟ་བུར་ལྟོས།།

རེས་འགའ་ཕ་མར་ཕྲད་ན་འདོད།།
ཕ་མར་ཕྲད་ན་འདོད་པའི་ཚེ།།
འགྲོ་ཀུན་དྲིན་ཅན་ཕ་མར་སྒོམས།།
ཕ་མ་སྒྱུ་མ་ལྟ་བུར་ལྟོས།།

རེས་འགའ་གྲོགས་དང་འགྲོགས་ན་འདོད།།
གྲོགས་དང་འགྲོགས་ན་འདོད་པའི་ཚེ།།
གྲོགས་སུ་བྱ་དང་རི་དྭགས་འགྲོགས།།
གྲོགས་རྣམས་སྒྱུ་མ་ལྟ་བུར་ལྟོས།།

Now and then I desire wealth,
And when I desire it,
I should accumulate the seven noble riches instead,
And see wealth and riches as illusions.

Occasionally I get homesick,
And when I get homesick,
I should take the palace of *dharmadhātu* as my home,
And see my homeland as an illusion.

At times I miss my parents,
And when I miss them,
I should think of all beings as kind parents,
And see my own parents as illusions.

Now and then I miss my friends,
And when I miss them,
I should make friends with the birds and wild hoofed animals,
And see my human friends as illusions.

རིས་འགག་བླ་མར་མཇལ་ན་འདོད།།
བླ་མར་མཇལ་ན་འདོད་པའི་ཚེ།།
འབྲལ་མེད་སྤྱི་བོ་སྙིང་དབུས་སྒོམས།།
བླ་མ་སྒྱུ་མ་ལྟ་བུར་ལྟོས།།

ཟླ་མེད་མི་ལ་རས་པ་ལ།།
གསོལ་བ་བཏབ་ནས་གླུ་འདི་བླངས།།
མི་ལ་རས་པའི་བྱིན་རླབས་ཀྱིས།།
རི་བ་གསར་བར་ཕན་པར་ཤོག།

ཅེས་པ་འདི་ཡང་ཚོགས་དྲུག་རང་གྲོལ་གྱིས་སྨྲས་པའོ།།

Sometimes I want to meet my lama,
And when I want to meet him, I should realize he is inseparable
from me,
At the crown of my head and in the middle of my heart,
And see the lama as an illusion.

I have prayed to the unrivaled Milarepa,
And have sung this song.
May Milarepa's blessing
Benefit all who will dwell in the mountains.

Tshogdruk Rangdrol also said this.

དྲིན་ཅན་བླ་མ་རྣམས་ལ་གསོལ་བ་འདེབས།།
མི་རྟག་འཆི་བ་དྲན་པར་བྱིན་གྱིས་རློབས།།
ཚེ་འདི་བློ་ཡིས་ཐོངས་པར་བྱིན་གྱིས་རློབས།།
དབེན་པར་ལྷ་ཆོས་ནུས་པར་བྱིན་གྱིས་རློབས།།

གྲུབ་དབང་མི་ལ་རས་པ་ལ་སོགས་པའི།།
སྔོན་བྱོན་དམ་པ་གོང་མའི་རྣམ་ཐར་བཞིན།།
མིང་དང་དོན་གཉིས་མཐུན་པའི་བྱ་བཏང་ཞིག།
བྱེད་པའི་དུས་ཤིག་བདག་ལ་ནམ་འོང་ཨང་།།

སྤང་ཕྱོངས་ནགས་ཚལ་མེ་ཏོག་རྒྱན་ལྡན་ཞིང་།།
ཆུ་གཙང་རྒྱུན་འབབ་བྱ་བྱིའུ་སྐད་སྙན་སྒྲོག།
ན་བུན་ལྡང་བའི་དབེན་པའི་དགའ་ཚལ་དུ།།
གཅིག་པུར་འདུག་པའི་དུས་ཤིག་ནམ་འོང་ཨང་།།

སྒྲུབ་པའི་དུས་སུ་དཀའ་ཚེགས་དཀའ་ལས་མྱུང་།།
སྤྱད་པས་མི་ངོམས་སྡིག་སྡུག་གཏམ་ངན་གསུམ།།

I pray to you, kind lamas:
Please bless me, that I may recall impermanence and death.
Please bless me, that I may renounce concerns for this life.
Please bless me, that I may be able to practice the divine Dharma
in solitary places.

Acting in harmony with the name "renunciant" and the two purposes,
As in the life stories of the holy forefathers,
Like the lord of siddhas, Milarepa—
Well then, when will that time come for me?

Living alone in meadows, forests, fields ornamented with flowers,
And lovely solitary groves
With rivers of pure water, birds calling out pleasingly, and
mist rising up—
Well then, when will that time come for me?

I am experiencing difficulties in my practice,
And I am not satisfied with my conduct.

སྣ་འདྲེན་ཤ་སོགས་ཞིམ་མངར་ཟས་སྤྲངས་ནས།།
ངན་ངོན་ཟ་བའི་དུས་ཤིག་ནམ་འོང་ཨང་།།

དད་ཟས་ལོག་འཚོ་མི་དགོས་ཤིག་སྲོ་མེད།།
ཚེ་རིང་ནད་མེད་རིག་པ་ཤིན་ཏུ་གསལ།།
ཉམས་རྟོགས་འཆར་སོགས་ཕན་ཡོན་མང་གསུངས་པས།།
བཙུད་ལེན་བྱེད་པའི་དུས་ཤིག་ནམ་འོང་ཨང་།།

དོན་མེད་རྣམ་གཡེང་གཏི་མུག་རོ་ཉལ་སྤྲངས།།
བླ་མའི་གདམས་ངག་རྩེ་གཅིག་ཉམས་སུ་བླངས།།
ཚེ་མཇུག་འདི་ལ་ས་ལམ་མཐར་ཕྱིན་ནས།།
གཞན་དོན་བྱེད་པའི་དུས་ཤིག་ནམ་འོང་ཨང་།།

ཞེས་པ་འདི་ཡང་སློབ་བུ་དོན་ཡོད་ཕུན་ཚོགས་ལ་བྱ་བཏང་ཚོགས་དྲུག་རང་གྲོལ་གྱིས་དབུས་ཀྱི་དབེན་གནས་ཟླ་ལུང་ནས་སྨྲས་པའོ།།

Renouncing evil, suffering, and harmful speech,
Delicious foods such as meat, which lead one astray,
And eating just a little bad food—
Well then, when will that time come for me?

The holy forefathers spoke of the benefits of
Not pursuing the perverted livelihood of eating food offered
by the faithful,
Not having lice or lice eggs,
Having a long life, being free from illness, having a very clear intellect,
Having profound experiences and realization, and so on.
Well then, when will that time come for me to make flower balls?

I have abandoned senseless distractions, delusions, and slothfulness.
I have practiced the oral instructions of my lama single-mindedly.
Well then, in what remains of this life, when will that time come for me
To reach the end of the ten *bhūmi*s and benefit others?

I, the renunciant Tshogdruk Rangdrol, said this to my disciple Dönyö Phüntsog at the solitary hermitage Salung.

ལྷ་འདྲེ་གདུག་པ་ཅན་རྣམས་བཏུལ།།
བོད་ཁམས་བདེ་ལ་འགོད་མཛད་པའི།།
ཨོ་རྒྱན་པདྨ་འབྱུང་གནས་ལ།།
གསོལ་བ་འདེབས་སོ་བྱིན་གྱིས་རློབས།།

རིག་པའི་ཁྲིའུ་ཆུང་གཞོན་ནུ་ཁྱོད།།
མི་ལུས་རྩྭ་ཕྱུང་ལ་བརྟེན་ནས།།
ཁམས་གསུམ་འཁོར་བའི་བྲག་ཡོགས་ཀྱི།།
འདོད་ཡོན་ཤིང་སེལ་བླངས་ནས་ཟོས།།

ཟོས་ཀྱིན་འདོད་པ་ཇེ་ཆེར་སོང་།།
ཡུན་རིང་ཟ་ཞིང་བསྡོད་པའི་བར།།
ཉིན་མཚན་བྲི་བ་དཀར་ནག་གིས།།
རྩྭ་ཕྱུང་ཉག་མ་རེ་རེ་འཁྲེར།།

ནམ་ཞིག་རྩྭ་ཕྱུང་ཟད་པའི་ཚེ།།
ཐར་བའི་བདེ་སར་འགྲོ་འདོད་ཀྱང་།།
མར་གྱི་རྩ་བའི་ངན་སོང་གསུམ།།
ཆུ་བྲག་འཐབ་པའི་གཅོང་རོང་དུ།།
ལྟུང་ནས་སྡུག་བསྔལ་མྱོང་བར་ངེས།།

I pray to Pema Jungne of Ogyen,
Who tamed the hostile gods and demons,
And established the land of Tibet in happiness.
Please bless me.

Mind—you intelligent, small, young boy—
You reclined on a heap of grass,
Took fruit from the tree of sensory pleasures
By the rock of the lower three realms,
And have been eating it.

As you eat, you are craving more and more.
While you have been sitting there day and night eating and eating,
A white and black mouse
Has been carrying away blades of grass one by one.

You want to go to the blissful land of liberation,
But one day when the pile of grass is gone,
You will fall into a canyon with rocky rapids—
The lower three realms down below—
And you will certainly experience great suffering.

རིག་པའི་ཁྱེའུ་ཆུང་དང་རིང་བོ།།
ཙྭ་ཤུང་ཕྱེད་ཀ་ཚར་ཤུད་ཐལ།།
ད་ནི་སྡོད་པའི་དུས་མ་ཡིན།།
འདོད་ཡོན་སེལ་ལ་སུ་ཡིད་ཆགས།།

ཚུར་ཤོག་ཤེས་རབ་སྟོང་ཉིད་རྟ།།
སྣ་ཚོགས་ཐབས་ཀྱིས་སྒ་སྲབ་སྒློ།།
འཐེན་ལ་རྟ་བཟང་སྒོང་དུ་ཞོན།།

འབད་བརྩོན་ལྕུག་གིས་ཡང་ཡང་བྲབས།།
ཐར་པའི་ལམ་ལ་ཁྲེན་དུ་རྒྱུགས།།
ཚེ་འདིར་ཕྱི་མིག་མི་བལྟ་བར།།
བདེ་ཆེན་ཐར་པའི་གྲོང་ཁྱེར་སྙོགས།།

ཨོ་རྒྱན་པདྨ་འབྱུང་གནས་ལ།།
གསོལ་བ་བཏབ་ནས་བླུ་འདི་བླངས།།
ཨོ་རྒྱན་པདྨའི་བྱིན་རླབས་ཀྱིས།།
རང་གཞན་རྒྱུད་ལ་ཕན་པར་ཤོག།

Mind—you intelligent, young, oblivious boy—
Half of the grass has already been pulled out.
Now is not the time to sit there.
Who is infatuated with the fruit of sensory pleasures?

Come here, horse of wisdom and emptiness!
Young boy—skillfully put on the bridle and saddle, draw up the cinch,
And mount this excellent horse!

Urge him on again and again with the crop of exertion.
Gallop uphill on the path of liberation.
Head for the city of great bliss and liberation,
And do not look back at concerns for this life.

Praying to Pema Jungne of Ogyen,
I sang this song.
May benefit come to my mind-stream and that of others
Through the blessings of Pema of Ogyen.

Chapter Seven

Old Age

གསར་རྙིང་ཆོས་ལུགས་ཀུན་མཁྱེན་པའི།།
ཕ་ཆན་ཆོས་ཀྱི་རྒྱལ་པོ་ལ།།
བུ་ངས་རྒྱུན་དུ་གསོལ་བ་འདེབས།།
བསྟན་འགྲོར་ཕན་པར་བྱིན་གྱིས་རློབས།།

མཁའ་ལ་འཕྱོ་བའི་གཡུ་འབྲུག་ང་།།
ཆས་རང་ཟེ་བ་མ་ཉམས་འདུག།

ནགས་ཁྲོད་འཁྲིམ་པའི་རྒྱ་སྟག་དེ།།
ཆས་རང་ཐིག་ལེ་མ་ཉམས་འདུག།

ཛ་ལུང་འཁྲིམ་པའི་འབྲོང་བོ་དེ།།
ཆས་རང་རུ་ཟུར་མ་ཉམས་འདུག།

རྒྱལ་ཁམས་འཁྲིམ་པའི་རྣལ་འབྱོར་ང་།།
ཆས་རང་དབང་པོ་མ་ཉམས་འདུག།

བྱ་རྒྱལ་ཁྱུང་ཆེན་ཆས་ན་ཡང་།།
ང་དུང་ནམ་འཕང་བསྟོད་ལ་སྒྲོ།།

སྟོབས་ལྡན་གླང་ཆེན་ཆས་ན་ཡང་།།
ང་དུང་ཁུར་ཆེན་འཁུར་ལ་སྒྲོ།།

Elderly father, Chökyi Gyälpo,
All-knowing about the Dharma traditions new and old—
I, your son, continuously petition you.
Please give your blessings to benefit the teachings and beings.

Although I, a turquoise thunder-dragon who soars in the sky, am aged,
My claws have not been dulled.

Although the tiger who wanders in the forest is aged,
His vitality is undiminished.

Although the wild yak who wanders the rocky cliffs is aged,
His horns have not worn down.

Although I, a yogi who strolls around the country, am aged,
My faculties are unimpaired.

Although the king of birds, the *garuḍa*, is aged,
He still delights in the heights of the sky.

Although the mighty elephant is aged,
He still delights in carrying heavy loads.

རྟ་མཆོག་ཅང་ཤེས་རྟས་ན་ཡང་།།
ང་དྲུང་ཞང་ཆེན་གཅོད་ལ་སྤྲོ།།

རྣལ་འབྱོར་ཞབས་དཀར་རྟས་ན་ཡང་།།
ང་དྲུང་འགྲོ་དོན་བྱེད་ལ་སྤྲོ།།

དེང་ནས་ཚེ་རབས་ཐམས་ཅད་དུ།།
ཕན་བདེའི་འབྱུང་གནས་བསྟན་པ་དང་།།
མར་གྱུར་སེམས་ཅན་ཐམས་ཅད་ལ།།
ཕན་ཐོགས་དཔག་མེད་འབྱུང་བར་ཤོག།

ཅེས་པ་འདི་ནི་དད་ཅན་འཁའ་རེས་ཁོང་དགུང་ལོ་མཐོ་རུང་དབང་པོ་གསལ་ཞིང་འགྲོ་དོན་བྱེད་པར་སྤྲོ་བ་བཀའ་དྲིན་ཆེ་བར་གདའ་ཟེར་དུས་རང་གི་ཡིད་ལ་ཤར་བ་ལྟར་སྨྲས་པའོ།།

Although the most excellent, omniscient horse is aged,
He still delights in cutting across a vast plain.

Although the yogi Shabkar is aged,
He still delights in acting for the benefit of beings.

From now on, through all my lifetimes,
May I be of unlimited service
To the teachings—the source of benefit and happiness—
And to all sentient beings, my mothers in all lifetimes.

Shabkar said this, according to whatever came to mind, when several of the faithful remarked that although he is aged, his faculties are still clear, he delights in acting for the welfare of beings, and he is very kind.

ཚར་དང་ཁ་བ་གཉིས་ཀྱིས།།
རང་གི་མགོ་ལ་གནོད་བྱུང་།།
ཡར་ལ་བཀག་པས་མ་ཐོག།
ཞྭ་ཞིག་གྱོན་པས་ཕན་སོང་།།

རྡོ་དང་ཚེར་མ་གཉིས་ཀྱིས།།
རང་གི་རྐང་ལ་གནོད་བྱུང་།།
མར་ལ་བསལ་བས་མ་ཚར།།
ལྷམ་ཞིག་གྱོན་པས་ཕན་སོང་།།

རྫུན་དང་ཚིག་རྩུབ་གཉིས་ཀྱིས།།
རང་གི་སེམས་ལ་གནོད་བྱུང་།།
ཕར་ལ་ལན་བྱས་མ་ཐུབ།།
བཟོད་པ་བསྒོམས་པས་ཕན་བྱུང་།།

མར་དང་འོ་མའི་གཞི་མ།།
འདོད་འཇོའི་བ་མོ་ཇྲས་རུང་།།
ད་དུང་འོ་མ་བཞོས་པས།།
མར་ཡང་མང་པོ་ཡོན་སོང་།།

Rain and snow both
Hurt my head.
I could not block each drop and flake.
I benefited by wearing a hat.

Stones and thorns both
Hurt my feet.
I could not avoid each stone and thorn.
I benefited by wearing shoes.

Lies and harsh words both
Hurt my mind.
I was not able to reply to each lie and insult.
I benefited by meditating on forgiveness.

The wish-fulfilling cow—
The source of butter and milk—has grown old.
But by milking her,
I still get lots of butter.

ས་ལམ་བགྲོད་པའི་གཞི་མ།།
ཅང་ཤེས་རྟ་མཆོག་རྒྱས་རྫུང་།།
ད་དུང་ཞོན་ནས་སོང་བས།།
ཐག་རིང་མང་བོ་འཁོར་སོང་།།

ལྷ་ཆོས་བྱེད་པའི་གཞི་མ།།
དཔལ་འབྱོར་མི་ལུས་རྒྱས་རྫུང་།།
ད་དུང་སྒོམ་སྒྲུབ་བྱས་པས།།
ཉམས་རྟོགས་མང་བོ་ཤར་སོང་།།

The omniscient horse—

The means for traversing the paths and stages—has grown old.

But by riding it,

I still travel through many distant places.

This human body with its freedoms and advantages—

The condition for performing the divine Dharma—has become aged.

But when I meditate and practice,

Many profound experiences and realizations are still coming forth.

ཞིང་འདི་ཡི་གདུལ་བྱ་སྨིན་གྲོལ་བཀོད།།
ཞིང་མང་པོའི་ལྷ་ཡིས་བསུ་སྐྱེལ་མཛད།།
ཞིང་གཞན་ག་ཤེགས་ཆོས་རྒྱལ་དག་དབང་ལྷང་།།
ཞིང་གང་ན་བཞུགས་ཀྱང་བུ་ལ་གཟིགས།།

མཚོ་དབྱར་དུས་དར་ཞིང་རྒྱས་པའི་ཚེ།།
རྒྱན་ཆུ་བྱ་ཕོ་མོས་བྱས་པས་མཛེས།།
དགུན་འཁྲམ་དར་རིམ་གྱིས་ཆགས་ཙ་ན།།
རྒྱན་ཆུ་བྱ་ཕོ་མོ་བྲལ་ནས་ཐལ།།

ཤིང་ཡལ་ག་ལོ་མ་རྒྱས་པའི་ཚེ།།
རྒྱན་མེ་ཏོག་འབྲས་བུས་བྱས་པས་མཛེས།།
སྟོན་སེར་སྐྱར་རིམ་གྱིས་སོང་ཙ་ན།།
རྒྱན་མེ་ཏོག་འབྲས་བུ་བྲལ་ནས་ཐལ།།

རང་གཞོན་ནུ་ཤ་ཁྲག་རྒྱས་པའི་ཚེ།།
རྒྱན་བླ་མ་ཕ་མས་བྱས་པས་མཛེས།།
ད་སྟོབས་མདངས་རིམ་གྱིས་ཉམས་ཙ་ན།།
རྒྱན་བླ་མ་ཕ་མ་བྲལ་ནས་ཐལ།།

You established the ripening and liberation of those to be tamed
in this realm.
Deities welcome and escort you in many realms.
Chögyäl Ngakyi Wang, who has departed for another realm,
Please look upon your spiritual son from whatever realm in which
you dwell.

In summer when the lake was large,
Pairs of waterbirds adorned it and made it beautiful.
In winter when ice encroached upon the shore,
The birds departed, and the beauty had passed by.

When the foliage on the trees was lush,
Flowers and fruit enhanced them and made them beautiful.
In the fall when the leaves were turning pale yellow,
The flowers and fruit were gone, and the beauty had passed by.

In my youth when my body was growing,
My lamas and parents enriched my life and made it beautiful.
Now, when my strength and vitality are declining,
My lamas and parents are gone: those who enriched my life
have passed by.

ཆོས་ཐམས་ཅད་མི་རྟག་འདི་དང་འདྲ།།
ཆོས་གསུང་མཁན་བླ་མའི་བཀའ་བཞིན་དུ།།
ཆོས་མྱུར་དུ་སྒྲུབས་དང་རི་ཁྲོད་པ།།
ཆོས་སྒྲུབ་རྟེན་ལུས་འདི་རྒས་ནས་ཐལ།།

རི་རྨ་རྒྱལ་མགུལ་ནས་དགོང་དུས་ཤིག།
སེམས་སྐྱོ་བའི་རྟ་ཞིག་རྙེད་ནས་ཞོན།།
མགུར་སྙན་མོའི་ལྷུག་འདིས་བྲབས་པའི་མོད།།
ཆོས་ཟབ་རྒྱུའི་ལམ་ལ་ཁྱུར་ནས་ཐལ།།

All phenomena are impermanent like this.
Practice the Dharma immediately, mountain hermit,
In accordance with the instructions of your lama.
This body, a necessary support for practicing the Dharma, has aged,
and is passing by.

One evening, on the slope of the mountain Magyäl,
I found a horse of disillusionment with the world, and am riding it.
At this very moment as I am urging him on with this crop
of a well-sounding *gur,*
He is carrying me on the path of deep, vast spirituality,
and is passing by.

Chapter Eight

Self-Criticism

རྗེ་རྒྱལ་ཀུན་སྤྱི་གཟུགས་པདྨ་འབྱུང་།།
བདག་སྣང་ངོར་ཐ་མལ་ཚུལ་འཛིན་པ།།
ཕ་བཀའ་དྲིན་གསུམ་ལྡན་ཆོས་ཀྱི་རྒྱལ།།
ཐུགས་བརྩེ་བའི་སྤྱན་གྱིས་གཟིགས་སུ་གསོལ།།

གྲོང་ཡུལ་ན་རྟག་ཏུ་སོ་ནམ་བྱེད།།
དགོན་ན་ཡང་ཚོང་དང་བུན་བསྐྱེད་བྱེད།།
དུས་དེང་སང་རི་ཁྲོད་འགྲིམས་ན་སྐྱིད།།
བདག་དབེན་པའི་དགའ་ཚལ་ཉམས་དགའ་བསྙེག།

གྲོང་ཡུལ་ན་ནོར་ཕྱིར་ལུས་སྲོག་གཏོང་།།
དགོན་ན་ཡང་ནོར་ཕྱིར་སྡོམ་པ་གཏོང་།།
དུས་དེང་སང་རི་ཁྲོད་འགྲིམས་ན་སྐྱིད།།
བདག་དབེན་པའི་དགའ་ཚལ་ཉམས་དགའ་བསྙེག།

གྲོང་ཡུལ་ན་ཚེ་འདི་དོན་དུ་གཉེར།།
དགོན་ན་ཡང་ཆོས་བརྒྱད་དོན་དུ་གཉེར།།
དུས་དེང་སང་རི་ཁྲོད་འགྲིམས་ན་སྐྱིད།།
བདག་དབེན་པའི་དགའ་ཚལ་ཉམས་དགའ་བསྙེག།

Oh father Chökyi Gyäl, possessed of the three kindnesses—
Though you have taken on the ways of an ordinary man,
I perceive you as Pema Jungne, embodiment of all lords,
the Victorious Ones.
I pray that you look upon me with eyes of affection.

In the village, I always engage in farming.
Even in the monastery, I engage in business and usury.
These days if I wandered among mountain hermitages,
I would be happy.
I will hasten to a pleasing, solitary grove.

In the village, I give life and limb for the sake of wealth.
Even in the monastery, I break my vows for wealth.
These days if I wandered among mountain hermitages,
I would be happy.
I will hasten to a pleasing, solitary grove.

In the village, I take pains for the sake of this life.
Even in the monastery, I take pains for the eight worldly concerns.
These days if I wandered among mountain hermitages,
I would be happy.
I will hasten to a pleasing, solitary grove.

གྲོང་ཡུལ་ན་འཐབ་རྩོད་འཁྲུག་ལོང་བྱེད།།
དགོན་ན་ཡང་ཕན་ཚུན་ཕྲག་དོག་བྱེད།།
དུས་དེང་སང་རི་ཁྲོད་འགྲིམས་ན་སྐྱིད།།
བདག་དབེན་པའི་དགའ་ཚལ་ཉམས་དགའ་བསྟེག།

གྲོང་ཡུལ་ན་མི་དགེའི་སྡིག་ལ་ཛམས།།
དགོན་ན་ཡང་འདོད་ཡོན་དཀོར་ལ་ཛམས།།
དུས་དེང་སང་རི་ཁྲོད་འགྲིམས་ན་སྐྱིད།།
བདག་དབེན་པའི་དགའ་ཚལ་ཉམས་དགའ་བསྟེག།

གྲོང་ཡུལ་ན་བཟའ་ཚང་སྐྱོང་དགོས་མང་།།
དགོན་ན་ཡང་དགོན་པའི་སྐྱོང་ཁུར་མང་།།
དུས་དེང་སང་རི་ཁྲོད་འགྲིམས་ན་སྐྱིད།།
བདག་དབེན་པའི་དགའ་ཚལ་ཉམས་དགའ་བསྟེག།

གྲོང་ཡུལ་ན་རྣམ་གཡེང་འདུ་འཛི་བྱེད།།
དགོན་ན་ཡང་ཆོས་མིན་བྱ་བ་བྱེད།།
དུས་དེང་སང་རི་ཁྲོད་འགྲིམས་ན་སྐྱིད།།
བདག་དབེན་པའི་དགའ་ཚལ་ཉམས་དགའ་བསྟེག།

In the village, I cause others to quarrel and fight.
Even in the monastery, I cause jealousy between others.
These days if I wandered among mountain hermitages,
    I would be happy.
I will hasten to a pleasing, solitary grove.

In the village, I crave evil practices.
Even in the monastery, I crave sensual pleasure and wealth.
These days if I wandered among mountain hermitages,
    I would be happy.
I will hasten to a pleasing, solitary grove.

In the village, I need to care for my family a lot.
Even in the monastery, I am burdened with responsibilities.
These days if I wandered among mountain hermitages,
    I would be happy.
I will hasten to a pleasing, solitary grove.

In the village, I am noisy and distract others.
Even in the monastery, I act contrary to the Dharma.
These days if I wandered among mountain hermitages,
    I would be happy.
I will hasten to a pleasing, solitary grove.

གྲོང་ཡུལ་ན་སྡུག་བསྔལ་མཚོ་ཆེན་བརྫོལ།།
དགོན་ན་ཡང་ཆགས་སྡང་ཆུ་མིག་བརྫོལ།།
དུས་དེང་སང་རི་ཁྲོད་འགྲིམས་ན་སྐྱིད།།
བདག་དབེན་པའི་དགའ་ཚལ་ཉམས་དགའ་བསྙེག།

རྗེ་བཀའ་གདམས་རྣམ་ཐར་སྐྱོང་འདོད་དང་།།
ཆོས་སྒྲུབ་པའི་རྒྱལ་མཚན་འཛིན་འདོད་རྣམས།།
དུས་དེང་སང་རི་ཁྲོད་འགྲིམས་ན་སྐྱིད།།
གནས་དབེན་པའི་དགའ་ཚལ་ཉམས་དགར་ཤོག།

ཆོས་སྙན་བརྒྱུད་བློ་སྦྱོང་སྐྱོང་འདོད་དང་།།
ཆོས་བྱང་ཆུབ་ལམ་རིམ་བསྒོམ་འདོད་རྣམས།།
དུས་དེང་སང་རི་ཁྲོད་འགྲིམས་ན་སྐྱིད།།
གནས་དབེན་པའི་དགའ་ཚལ་ཉམས་དགར་ཤོག།

ལམ་བསྐྱེད་རྫོགས་ཟབ་མོ་བསྒོམ་འདོད་དང་།།
ལམ་འོད་གསལ་རྫོགས་ཆེན་བསྒོམ་འདོད་རྣམས།།
དུས་དེང་སང་རི་ཁྲོད་འགྲིམས་ན་སྐྱིད།།
གནས་དབེན་པའི་དགའ་ཚལ་ཉམས་དགར་ཤོག།

In the village, the great lake of suffering overflows.
Even in the monastery, the spring of attraction and aversion overflows.
These days if I wandered among mountain hermitages,
  I would be happy.
I will hasten to a pleasing, solitary grove.

Those of you who want to emulate the lives of the Kadampa lords,
And who want to uphold the victory banner of Dharma practitioners,
If you wander these days among mountain hermitages,
  you will be happy.
Please come to a pleasing, solitary grove.

You who want to sustain the Oral Lineage and cultivate Mind Training,
And who want to train in the Stages of the Path of Enlightenment—
If you wander these days among mountain hermitages,
  you will be happy.
Please come to a pleasing, solitary grove.

You who want to cultivate the profound paths of the Generation Stage
  and Completion Stage,
And you who want to follow the path of Radiant Light, *Dzogchen*—
If you wander these days among mountain hermitages,
  you will be happy.
Please come to a pleasing, solitary grove.

ཚེ་འདི་ལ་ཕྱི་མིག་མི་བལྟ་བར།།
ཚེ་སྒྲུབ་པ་སྙོམས་འདོད་སྐལ་ལྡན་ཀུན།།
དུས་དེང་སང་རི་ཁྲོད་འགྲིམས་ན་སྐྱིད།།
གནས་དབེན་པའི་དགའ་ཚལ་ཉམས་དགར་ཤོག།

དགེ་འདིས་ཀྱང་རང་གཞན་ལ་ཕན་ནས།།
རྗེ་དམ་པ་གོང་མའི་རྣམ་ཐར་བཞིན།།
གནས་དབེན་པའི་དགའ་ཚལ་བསྙེན་ནས་ཀྱང་།།
ཆོས་ཉམས་སུ་བླངས་ནས་འཚང་རྒྱ་ཤོག།

ཅེས་པ་འདི་ཡང་ཚོགས་དྲུག་རང་གྲོལ་གྱིས་རང་ལ་སྨྲས་པའོ།།

All you fortunate ones who want to make life and practice one,
Without a backward glance at concerns for this life—
If you wander these days among mountain hermitages,
    you will be happy.
Please come to a pleasing, solitary grove.

May this merit benefit myself and others.
And keeping to a pleasing, solitary grove
Following the examples of the holy lords, our forefathers,
May we take spiritual practices to heart and attain enlightenment.

I, Tshogdruk Rangdrol, also said this to myself.

Chapter Nine

Nonsectarianism

ན་མོ་གུ་རུ།

ཡ་ཀི་སྟོང་གསལ་གྱི་ནམ་མཁའ་ཡངས་པ་ན།།
འོད་སྟོང་ཕྱོགས་བཅུ་རུ་འཕྲོ་བའི་ཉི་མ་ཁྱོད།།
འགྲོ་མགོན་སངས་རྒྱས་དེ་ཡིན་ན་དགའ་བ་ལ།།
བོད་ལ་ཆོས་འཁོར་ཞིག་བསྐོར་བར་བསྐུལ་ན་ཨང་།།

ལྷོ་ནུབ་ཕྱོགས་ཀྱི་རིའི་རྩེ་མོའི་ནམ་མཁའ་ན།།
འོ་མ་འཁྱུར་བ་བཞིན་ལྡིང་བའི་སྤྲིན་དཀར་ཁྱོད།།
པད་འབྱུང་ཡབ་སྲས་ཚོ་ཡིན་ན་སྐྱིད་པ་ལ།།
རྫོགས་པ་ཆེན་པོ་ཡི་ལྷ་ཁྲིད་ཞུས་ན་ཨང་།།

ཤར་ཕྱོགས་རི་བོ་ཡི་རྩེ་མོའི་ནམ་མཁའ་ན།།
ཞོ་གསར་སྤྲུངས་པ་བཞིན་ལངས་པའི་སྤྲིན་དཀར་ཁྱོད།།
མི་ལ་ཡབ་སྲས་ཚོ་ཡིན་ན་དགའ་བ་ལ།།
ཕྱག་རྒྱ་ཆེན་པོ་ཡི་ལྷ་ཁྲིད་ཞུས་ན་ཨང་།།

I bow to the lama.

You sun shining forth brilliantly in the ten directions
Of the broad sky empty and clear up above—
If you are the protector of beings, the Buddha—Oh joy!
Well! Then I entreat you to turn the wheel of the Dharma in Tibet!

You white clouds floating gently like milk boiling over
In the sky by the tips of the mountains to the southwest—
If you are Pema Jungne and his disciples—Oh happiness!
Well! Then I request the instructions for *Dzogchen*.

You white clouds piling up like heaps of fresh yogurt
In the sky over the peaks of the eastern mountains—
If you are Milarepa and his disciples—Oh joy!
Well! Then I request the instructions for *Mahāmudrā*.

སྙིང་ཕྱོགས་ནམ་མཁའ་ན་དར་ཡུག་དཀར་པོ་ཞིག།
ཕྱོགས་བཞིར་བརྒྱངས་པ་ལྷར་འཕེན་པའི་སྤྲིན་དཀར་ཕྱོད།།
བློ་བཟང་ཡབ་སྲས་ཚོ་ཡིན་ན་སྐྱིད་པ་ལ།།
དབུ་མ་ཆེན་མོ་ཡི་ལྷ་ཁྲིད་ཞུས་ན་ཨང་།།

ཞེས་པ་འདི་ནི་ཉིན་ཞིག་སྤུ་རྡོ་ཕྱོགས་ཕྱོགས་ནས་སྤྲིན་ལངས་པ་དང་ལྡིང་བ་མཐོང་ཚེ་
གངས་དཀར་རི་བོ་རྨ་ཆེན་ནས་བླངས་པའོ།།

You white clouds stretching out like a white banner
Unfurling in the four directions of the sky overhead—
If you are Lobzang Dragpa and his disciples—Oh happiness!
Well! Then I request the instructions for the great *Madhyamaka.*

I sang this one afternoon at the white snow-covered mountain, Machen, when I saw clouds rising and floating in every direction.

འོད་གསལ་ཉིམ་དེ་ནམ་མཁར་ཤར།།
འོད་ཀྱིས་ཕྱོགས་མཚམས་ཀུན་ཁྱབ་པ་མཐོང་།།
ཨོ་རྒྱན་པདྨ་དེ་བོད་དུ་བྱོན།།
རྒྱལ་བསྟན་བཙུགས་པའི་ཚུལ་ཡིད་ལ་ཤར།།

བྱ་རྒྱལ་རྒོད་པོ་ཞིག་མདུན་མཁར་འོངས།།
ནམ་མཁར་ཡར་ཡར་དུ་བསྐྱོད་པ་མཐོང་།།
གྲུབ་ཆེན་མི་ལ་ཁོང་བོད་དུ་བྱོན།།
གྲུབ་རྟགས་བསྟན་པའི་ཚུལ་ཡིད་ལ་ཤར།།

དངུལ་དཀར་མདོག་འདྲའི་སྤྲིན་ནམ་མཁར་འཁྲིགས།།
སྤྲང་ཆར་འཇམ་པོ་ཞིག་བབས་པ་མཐོང་།།
ཇོ་བཙུན་ཙོང་ཁ་པ་བོད་དུ་བྱོན།།
ཆོས་ཆར་ཕབ་པའི་ཚུལ་ཡིད་ལ་ཤར།།

འཛམ་གླིང་ཉིམ་དེ་འོད་ལམ་ལམ།།
ནུབ་ཕྱོགས་རི་སྐྱིབས་སུ་ཡིབས་པ་མཐོང་།།
སྐྱོབ་དཔོན་པད་འབྱུང་ཁོང་ཟངས་མདོག་གི།
དཔལ་རིར་གཞིགས་པའི་ཚུལ་ཡིད་ལ་ཤར།།

Shining with radiant clarity, the sun rose.
I saw the light pervade the whole compass of the sky.
The way Pema of Ogyen arrived in Tibet
And established the teaching of the Victorious Ones came to mind.

An eagle, king of birds, appeared before me in the sky.
I saw him climb higher and higher.
The way the *mahāsiddha* Milarepa arrived in Tibet
And displayed signs of accomplishment came to mind.

Clouds the color of silver gathered in the sky.
I saw a soft rain gently fall.
The way the venerable Tsongkhapa arrived in Tibet
And made the rain of the Dharma fall came to mind.

I saw the dazzling light, that sun of the world,
Take shelter at the mountain refuge of the west.
The way the spiritual master Pema Jungne departed
For the Glorious Copper-Colored Mountain came to mind.

བྱ་རྒྱལ་རྒོད་པོ་ཡིས་འདབ་གཤོག་བརྒྱངས།།
བཞུད་ནས་ཕར་ཕྱོགས་སྤུ་འགྲོ་བ་མཐོང་།།
སྒྲུབ་ཆེན་མི་ལ་ཁོང་མདོན་དགའ་ཡི།།
ཞིང་དུ་གཤེགས་པའི་ཚུལ་ཡིད་ལ་ཤར།།

དངུལ་དཀར་མདོག་འདྲའི་སྤྲིན་གཡོ་འགྱུལ་བྱས།།
སྙིང་ཕྱོགས་ནམ་མཁའ་ལ་ཐིམ་པ་མཐོང་།།
རྗེ་བཙུན་སྒྲོ་བཟང་ཁོང་དགའ་ལྡན་གྱི།།
ཞིང་དུ་གཤེགས་པའི་ཚུལ་ཡིད་ལ་ཤར།།

འཆི་མེད་རྡོ་རྗེ་ཡི་སྐུ་བརྙེས་ཀྱང་།།
རྟག་འཛིན་ཅན་རྣམས་ཆོས་བསྐུལ་ཕྱིར་དུ།།
འགྲོ་མགོན་དེ་གསུམ་གྱིས་མི་རྟག་པའི།།
རྣམ་འགྱུར་བསྟན་པའི་ཚུལ་ཡིད་ལ་ཤར།།

རང་ལུས་མི་རྟག་པར་འཇིག་པར་ངེས།།
འཇིག་རྟེན་མི་ཆོས་སྤྲངས་ཆོས་བསྒྲུབས་ནས།།
ཕྱི་མ་འགྲོ་མགོན་གསུམ་བཞུགས་པའི་ཞིང་།།
གསུམ་དུ་འགྲོ་འདོད་ཅིག་ཡིད་ལ་ཤར།།

ཞེས་པ་འདི་ཡང་ཕྱི་རོལ་གྱི་སྣང་བས་རྐྱེན་བྱས་ནས་ཡིད་ལ་ཤར་བ་ལྟར་གངས་རིའི་ར་བ་ནས་བླངས་པའོ།།

The eagle, king of birds, spread its wings and departed.
I saw him head off toward the east.
The way the *mahāsiddha* Milarepa departed
For the Pure Realm of Abhirati came to mind.

The silver clouds stirred.
I saw them dissolve into the sky overhead.
The way the reverend Lobzang Dragpa departed
For the Pure Realm of Ganden came to mind.

Although they had attained immortal *vajra* bodies,
The way those three protectors of beings
Displayed a transitory appearance in order to urge
Those clinging to permanence to follow the Dharma came to mind.

It is certain that my transitory body will be destroyed.
A desire to abandon worldly ways, practice the Dharma,
And be reborn in the three Pure Realms
Where the three protectors of beings reside came to mind.

I sang this in accordance with memories inspired by external appearances at a range of snow-covered mountains.

ང་འགྲོ་ང་འགྲོ་དབེན་པའི་སྤྲང་ལ་འགྲོ།།
སྤྲང་ག་ཤོངས་མི་ཧོག་བཀྲ་བའི་ལྗོངས་སུ་འགྲོ།།
སྒོ་ལྷན་སྐྱིད་དུ་བདེ་བར་ཉལ་དུ་འགྲོ།།
བུང་བས་སྒྲ་དབྱངས་སྒྲོག་ལ་ཉན་དུ་འགྲོ།།

ང་འགྲོ་ང་འགྲོ་དབེན་པའི་གནས་ལ་འགྲོ།།
ལྗོན་ཤིང་འདབ་རྒྱས་བསིལ་གྲིབ་བསྟེན་དུ་འགྲོ།།
ཞིམ་པའི་སིལ་ཧོག་མང་པོ་ཟ་རུ་འགྲོ།།
ཁུ་བྱུག་སྐད་སྙན་སྒྲོག་ལ་ཉན་དུ་འགྲོ།།

ང་འགྲོ་ང་འགྲོ་དབེན་པའི་རྫ་ལ་འགྲོ།།
རྫ་རི་ཁྲ་མོའི་སྒྲུབ་ཕུག་བསྟེན་དུ་འགྲོ།།
དྭངས་བསིལ་རྟོག་མེད་རྫ་ཆུ་འཐུང་དུ་འགྲོ།།
རི་དྭགས་རྒྱ་བྲོ་བརྡུང་ལ་བལྟ་རུ་འགྲོ།།

ང་འགྲོ་ང་འགྲོ་དབེན་པའི་བྲག་ལ་འགྲོ།།
བྲག་དམར་བྱ་རྒོད་ལྡིང་བའི་རྒྱ་རུ་འགྲོ།།
མ་བྱས་རང་གྲུབ་བྲག་ཕུག་བསྟེན་དུ་འགྲོ།།
ཟྭ་དང་སྒྲོག་སོགས་ཚོད་མ་ཟ་རུ་འགྲོ།།

I'm going, I'm going, I'm going to a solitary meadow.
I'm going to a valley where meadow flowers are blooming.
I'm going to lie comfortably on green, damp grass.
I'm going to hear the bees buzzing their songs.

I'm going, I'm going, I'm going to a solitary place.
I'm going to stay under the cool shade of lush trees.
I'm going to eat a lot of delicious fruit.
I'm going to hear cuckoos calling out clearly.

I'm going, I'm going, I'm going to a solitary clay mountain.
I'm going to stay in a meditation cave on a colorful mountain.
I'm going to drink the clear, cool, pure water that flows among the mountain's rocks.
I'm going to watch the wild hoofed animals playing, dancing, and sparring.

I'm going, I'm going, I'm going to a solitary rock.
I'm going to a red rock peak around which a vulture is soaring.
I'm going to stay in a natural cave for practicing the Dharma.
I'm going to eat vegetables such as nettles and garlic.

ང་འགྲོ་ང་འགྲོ་དབེན་གནས་གང་དགར་འགྲོ།།
དམ་པ་གོང་མའི་རྣམ་ཐར་སྐྱོང་དུ་འགྲོ།།
སྒྲུབ་བརྒྱུད་བསྟན་པའི་རྒྱལ་མཚན་འཛིན་དུ་འགྲོ།།
སྒྱུ་མའི་ལུས་པོ་རི་ལ་འཛོག་ཏུ་འགྲོ།།

ང་འགྲོ་ང་འགྲོ་ད་ནི་སྨྱུར་དུ་འགྲོ།།
ཕ་ཡུལ་བཙོན་ར་རྒྱབ་ཏུ་བཞག་ནས་འགྲོ།།
བཙོན་སྲུང་གཉེན་ལ་ལྷག་པ་བསྟན་ནས་འགྲོ།།
ཆགས་སྡང་སྨྲེ་སྔགས་འདོན་འཕྲོ་བཞག་ལ་འགྲོ།།

ང་འགྲོ་ང་འགྲོ་འགྲོ་ན་འདི་ལྟར་འགྲོ།།
སྦྲ་དབྱུག་བཟང་པོའི་རྟ་པོ་ཞོན་བཞིན་འགྲོ།།
དག་ནས་སྙན་པའི་གླུ་དབྱངས་ལེན་བཞིན་འགྲོ།།
སེམས་ལ་བླ་མའི་གདམས་ངག་དྲན་བཞིན་འགྲོ།།

དབུ་མ་ཉམས་སུ་ལེན་རྣམས་ང་བཞིན་གྱིས།།
རྫོགས་ཆེན་ཉམས་སུ་ལེན་རྣམས་ང་བཞིན་གྱིས།།
ཕྱག་ཆེན་ཉམས་སུ་ལེན་རྣམས་ང་བཞིན་གྱིས།།
མདོར་ན་ལྷ་ཆོས་བྱེད་རྣམས་ང་བཞིན་གྱིས།།

ཞེས་པ་འདི་ཡང་རེབ་གོང་བླ་བ་ཚོགས་དྲུག་རང་གྲོལ་གྱིས་ཕྱོགས་མེད་རི་ཁྲོད་འཁྱིམ་པའི་དུས་ཤིག་ཏུ་བླངས་པའོ།།

I'm going, I'm going, I'm going to any joyful hermitage.
I'm going to emulate the lives of the holy forefathers.
I'm going to hoist the victory banner of the teachings of the
Practice Lineage.
I'm going to place this illusory body on a mountain.

I'm going, I'm going, now I'm quickly going.
Leaving the prison—my homeland—behind, I'm going.
Showing the prison guards—my kinsmen—the nape of my neck,
I'm going.
Leaving behind the weeping over loves and hates, I'm going.

I'm going, I'm going, and while going, I'm going in this way:
Riding the stallion of my good walking stick, I'm going.
Singing a pleasing song with my voice, I'm going.
Recalling the lama's oral instructions, I'm going.

You who practice *Madhyamaka*—do as I do.
You who practice *Dzogchen*—do as I do.
You who practice *Mahāmudrā*—do as I do.
In short, you who practice the divine Dharma—do as I do.

I, the Rebgong singer Tshogdruk Rangdrol, sang this one time when I was wandering aimlessly among mountain hermitages.

Chapter Ten

Hermitage

ཉི་ཟླ་བཞིན་དུ་རི་ཁྲོད་འགྲིམས།།
སེང་གེ་བཞིན་དུ་ཉམ་ང་མེད།།
བྱ་རྒོད་བཞིན་དུ་ཆགས་པ་མེད།།
དེ་འདྲའི་སྐྱེས་བུ་རྣམས་ལ་འདུད།།

མི་ནག་གྲོང་བའི་ཁྲིམ་འདི་ན།།
ཞེ་སྡང་ཐབ་ནང་མེ་བཞིན་འབར།།
འདོད་ཆགས་ཟངས་ནང་ཇ་བཞིན་ཁོལ།།
གཏི་མུག་དུད་པ་བཞིན་དུ་འཐུལ།།
སེར་སྣ་ཟ་མའི་ཁ་བཞིན་དམ།།
ཕྲག་དོག་སློ་ཡི་ཁྲི་བཞིན་ཟུག།
ང་རྒྱལ་ཁྲིམ་གྱི་གླང་བཞིན་འཕུན།།
སྡུག་བསྔལ་བཟའ་བཏུང་བཞིན་དུ་མང་།།

ཕ་ཡུལ་སྡུག་བསྔལ་རྒྱ་མཚོ་ནས།།
བག་ཕེབས་སྤྱོད་པ་མ་སྨྱོས་སམ།།

འགྲོ་ན་དམ་པ་གོང་མ་བཞིན།།
ཡིད་འོང་དབེན་པའི་གནས་ལ་གཤེགས།།

They have wandered around mountain hermitages like the sun
and moon.
They are fearless, like the lion.
They are detached, like the vulture.
I bow to people like that.

As for you laypeople in this village home,
Your anger burns like fire in a hearth.
Your lust boils like tea in a cauldron.
Your delusion spreads everywhere like smoke.
Your greed is unyielding, like a mouth filled with food.
Your envy pierces, like a watchdog's fangs.
Your arrogance grunts, like the household cow.
And you indulge in suffering as if it were food and drink.

Hasn't it been crazy to stay so at ease
In your homeland, an ocean of suffering?

If you go somewhere,
Go to an enchanting solitary place like the holy forefathers did.

ལྗོན་ཤིང་གར་སྐྱབས་བྱེད་པའི་གསེབ།།
སྤང་རི་མེ་ཏོག་བཀྲ་བའི་ལྗོངས།།
བུང་བ་ལང་ཡིང་འཕུར་བའི་སྐྱིབས།།
བྱ་སྐད་མང་པོ་སྒྲོག་པའི་ས།།
རི་དྭགས་རྩེད་བྲོ་བརྡུང་བའི་གནས།།
ཛ་ཆུ་ལྡུང་ལྡུང་འབབ་པའི་རི།།
ངོ་མཚར་དབེན་པའི་ནགས་ཁྲོད་ན།།
ཤིང་ཐོག་རྣམ་པ་སྣ་ཚོགས་པ།།
ཁྱིམ་པའི་གྲོ་ནས་བཞིན་དུ་མོད།།

ཟླ་དང་སྒྲོག་སྔོའི་ཚོད་མ་རྣམས།།
ཁྱིམ་པའི་ལོ་ཡི་རྩྭ་བཞིན་མོད།།

རབ་མཛེས་བྱ་དང་རི་དྭགས་རྣམས།།
ཁྱིམ་པ་ཕོ་མོ་ལས་ཀྱང་མཛེས།།

རྒྱུན་དུ་འགྲོགས་ན་ཞེ་རྒྱུད་ནི།།
ཁྱིམ་པ་ཕོ་མོ་ལས་ཀྱང་འཇམ།།

སྐད་རིག་སྣ་ཚོགས་འབྱིན་པ་ནི།།
ཁྱིམ་པའི་གླིང་བུ་ལས་ཀྱང་སྙན།།

Above a valley covered with green meadows
Where flowers blaze with color among dancing trees,
A shelter where bees fly about, gently drifting,
Birds sing melodiously,
And deer play, dance, and spar
There is a wondrous, solitary forest
On a mountain whose gurgling streams fall among rocks
Where many kinds of fruit
Are as plentiful as a householder's wheat and barley.

Vegetables—nettles and green leeks—
Are abundant, like a householder's crops.

The birds and deer
Are even more beautiful than male and female householders.

They continually befriend you,
And their affections are even more tender than those between
man and woman.

The various tongues that are spoken there
Sound even more pleasing than a householder's flute.

མ་རིག་ཉོན་མོངས་དུག་ལྔ་རྣམས།།
ཁྱིམ་པའི་གསེར་དངུལ་བཞིན་དུ་དཀོན།།

ཉིན་རེ་བཞིན་གྱི་དགེ་སྦྱོར་ནི།།
ཁྱིམ་པའི་སྟོན་ཐོག་ལས་ཀྱང་མང་།།

ཉམས་དང་རྟོགས་པའི་ཡོན་ཏན་ནི།།
ཁྱིམ་པའི་ལོ་ལེགས་བཞིན་དུ་སྐྱེ།།

ཁྱིམ་ལས་དབེན་པ་འཕགས་པའི་ཚུལ།།
བཤད་ན་བརྗོད་ཀྱིས་མི་ལང་ངོ་།།

ཁྱིམ་གྱི་རབ་འབར་མེ་འོབས་སུ།།
ནན་གྱིས་སྡོད་པ་མ་འཁྲུལ་ལམ།།
རི་ཁྲོད་དབེན་པའི་བསིལ་གྲིབ་ཏུ།།
ད་ལྟ་བསྡད་ན་མི་ལེགས་སམ།།

ཁྱིམ་གྱི་གཏིང་ཟབ་ཚུ་ཆེན་དུ།།
མི་ཚུགས་སྡོད་པ་སྨྱོས་སམ་ཅི།།
རི་ཁྲོད་དབེན་པའི་སྐམ་ས་རུ།།
ད་ལྟ་བདེ་བར་བསྡད་ན་ལེགས།།

Ignorance, obscuring emotions, and the five poisons
Are as rare as a householder's gold and silver.

Daily virtuous deeds
Are even more plentiful than a householder's harvest.

Qualities of profound experiences and realization
Grow like a householder's bounteous crop.

How a solitary place is more noble than a household
Cannot be explained in words.

Haven't you been deluded to stay so obstinately
In the blazing pit of a household?
Wouldn't it be good if you stayed instead
In the cool shade of a mountain hermitage?

Have you been crazy or what to remain
In the very deep current of a household, at its mercy?
It would be good if you stayed at ease now
On the dry shore of a mountain hermitage.

དཀོར་ཟས་དུག་ཆུ་བདུད་རྩི་བཞིན།།
ཉམས་བཞིན་སྤྱོད་པ་མ་འཁྲུལ་ལམ།།
རི་ཁྲོད་དབེན་པར་གཤེགས་ནས་ཀྱང་།།
དམ་ཆོས་བདུད་རྩི་འཐུང་ན་ལེགས།།

ཆོས་བརྒྱད་འཁོར་བའི་ཆུ་དཀྱིལ་ལྷུང་།།
སྡུག་བསྔལ་འོ་དོད་འབོད་པའི་མི།།
གླུ་དབྱངས་མཉན་པ་བཟང་པོ་འདིས།།
དབེན་པའི་སྐམ་སར་འཁྲིད་པར་ཤོག།

ཅེས་པ་འདི་ཡང་འཁོར་བའི་དུག་ཆུའི་ནང་དུ་སྡུག་བསྔལ་གྱིས་འཁྱེ་ཡོག་སྣ་ཚོགས་བྱེད་པ་རྣམས་དབེན་པའི་སྐམ་སར་ཨེ་ཡོན་སྙམ་ནས་གླུ་དབྱངས་མཉན་པ་འདི་བྱ་བཏང་ཁ་བདེ་སེམས་སྐྱིད་ཚོགས་དྲུག་རང་གྲོལ་གྱིས་བཏང་བའོ།།

Haven't you been deluded to enjoy
The food offerings when someone dies,
Craving this poison as if it were honey?
You should go to a mountain hermitage and drink the nectar
of spirituality.

You are falling right into the midst of the river of samsara
with its eight worldly concerns.
May the song by this good ferryman
Lead those people who are lamenting loudly about suffering
To the shores of a solitary place.

The ferryman-songster, the renunciant, articulate, happy Tshogdruk Rangdrol, sent this song out, wondering whether those whose suffering makes them roil in the poisons of samsara would reach the dry shores of a hermitage.

འོ་འོ་རྫོན་པ་ཁྲི་ཁྲིད་བསླེབས་ཐལ།།
ཨཙུ་ཤ་བ་སྨུག་པོ་མ་འདུག།
ཁོ་རེ་རྫ་རི་མཐོན་པོ་སྐོགས་དང་།།
ཧེ་ཧེ་བློ་བདེ་དཔལ་ཡིན་ཨེ་གོ།

འོ་འོ་བྲུ་ཁྲ་སྲིག་ཅན་བསླེབས་ཐལ།།
ཨཙུ་འདབ་ཆགས་བྲེའུ་མ་འདུག།
ཁོ་རེ་ཤིང་ནགས་མཐུག་པོ་སྐོགས་དང་།།
ཧེ་ཧེ་བློ་བདེ་དཔལ་ཡིན་ཨེ་གོ།

འོ་འོ་བྲི་ལ་གཡོ་ཅན་བསླེབས་ཐལ།།
ཨཙུ་བྲི་བ་སྨུག་རིལ་མ་འདུག།
ཁོ་རེ་བུ་ག་ཕུགས་རིང་སྐོགས་དང་།།
ཧེ་ཧེ་བློ་བདེ་དཔལ་ཡིན་ཨེ་གོ།

འོ་འོ་ཉ་བདའ་ངོ་ནག་བསླེབས་ཐལ།།
ཨཙུ་ཉ་མོ་གསེར་མིག་མ་འདུག།
ཁོ་རེ་མཚོ་ཡི་དཀྱིལ་དེ་སྐོགས་དང་།།
ཧེ་ཧེ་བློ་བདེ་དཔལ་ཡིན་ཨེ་གོ།

Oh yeah! The hunter, leading a dog, has arrived.
Hey you! You dark bay stag—don't stay.
Hey! Seek out a high slate mountain.
Ha ha! The mind at ease is glorious, get it?

Oh yeah! The sinful hawk has arrived.
Hey you! You little birds—don't stay.
Hey! Seek out a thick forest.
Ha ha! The mind at ease is glorious, get it?

Oh yeah! The deceitful cat has arrived.
Hey you! You round gray mice—don't stay.
Hey! Seek out a deep hole.
Ha ha! The mind at ease is glorious, get it?

Oh yeah! The mean fisherman has arrived.
Hey you! Female fish with golden eyes—don't stay.
Hey! Seek out the middle of a lake.
Ha ha! The mind at ease is glorious, get it?

འོ་འོ་སྒྲ་དཀར་གཅེར་མ་བསྒྲིབས་ཐལ།།
ཨའུ་བྲུ་བཏང་བན་རྐན་མ་འདུག།
ཁོ་རེ་རི་ཁྲོད་དབེན་པ་སྐྱོགས་དང་།།
ཧེ་ཧེ་སློ་བདེ་དཔལ་ཡིན་ཨེ་གོ།།

ཞེས་པ་འདི་ཡང་རྗེ་སྐལ་ལྡན་རས་པའི་གསུང་དང་མཐུན་པར་རེབ་གོང་སྐྱ་བ་ཚོགས་དྲུག་རང་གྲོལ་གྱིས་དབེན་པ་ལ་ཡིད་སྨོན་པའི་ཤུགས་ཀྱིས་སྨྲས་པའོ།།

Oh yeah!	White hair and wrinkles have arrived.
Hey you!	Old renunciant monk—don't stay.
Hey!	Seek out a mountain hermitage.
Ha ha!	The mind at ease is glorious, get it?

This also was spoken by the Rebgong songster, Tshogdruk Rangdrol, feeling moved by happiness and joy at a hermitage, in conformity with the words of the lord, Kälden Repa.

རྫོན་པ་ཁྲི་ཁྲིད་ནི་སླེབས་བྱུང་།།
ཤ་བ་སྨུག་པོ་ནི་འབྲོས་སོ།།
ཛ་རི་མཐོན་པོ་ནི་བཟང་ངོ།།

ང་རྒྱལ་སེང་གེ་ནི་སླེབས་བྱུང་།།
ཡོན་ཏན་རི་བོང་ནི་འབྲོས་ས།།
ཁེངས་སྐྱུངས་བྲག་ཕུག་ནི་བཟང་ངོ།།

བྱ་ཁྲ་སྡིག་ཅན་ནི་སླེབས་བྱུང་།།
འདབ་ཆགས་བྱིའུ་ནི་འབྲོས་ས།།
ཤིང་ནགས་འཐུག་པོ་ནི་བཟང་ངོ།།

དགོར་ཟས་མེ་ལྕེ་ནི་སླེབས་བྱུང་།།
དགེ་སེམས་རྩྭ་ཤིང་ནི་འབྲོས་ས།།
སྒྲིབ་སྒྲོང་འཁྲུག་པ་ནི་བཟང་ངོ།།

བྱི་ལ་གཡོ་ཅན་ནི་སླེབས་བྱུང་།།
རྐུན་མོ་བྱི་བ་ནི་འབྲོས་ས།།
བུག་པ་ཕུག་རིང་ནི་བཟང་ངོ།།

ལོག་རྟོག་ཁ་བ་ནི་སླེབས་བྱུང་།།
དད་པ་གཅེར་བུ་ནི་འབྲོས་ས།།
ལེགས་བཤད་རྩྭ་ནང་ནི་བཟང་ངོ།།

The hunter, leading a dog, arrived.
The place of refuge for the dark bay stag,
A high clay mountain, is good.

The proud lion arrived.
The place of refuge for the rabbit of qualities,
A cave for leaving arrogance behind, is good.

The sinful bird of prey arrived.
The place of refuge for the little bird,
A deep forest, is good.

The flame of the fire of wealth and food arrived.
The place of refuge for the grass and trees of virtuous mind,
A cool area for cleansing obscurations, is good.

The deceitful cat arrived.
The place of refuge for the thieving mouse,
The innermost part of a hole, is good.

The snow of false knowledge arrived.
The place of refuge for pure faith
Within the grass of eloquent speech is good.

ཉ་བ་རྒྱ་ཕྱོགས་ནི་སླེབས་བྱུང་།།
ཉ་མོ་སྒོང་སྐྱེས་ནི་འབྲོས་ས།།
གཏིང་ཟབ་ཆུ་ཆེན་ནི་བཟང་ངོ་།།

སྒྲ་དཀར་སོ་བ་ནི་སླེབས་བྱུང་།།
སྤྲང་ཆན་དབང་ཆུང་ནི་འབྲོས་ས།།
རི་ཁྲོད་དབེན་པ་ནི་བཟང་ངོ་།།

ཞེས་པ་འདི་ཡང་སྐལ་ལྡན་རྒྱ་མཚོས་སྦྱར་བའོ།།

The net of a fisherman arrived.
The place of refuge for the spawning of the fish,
Deep, vast water, is good.

The white-haired spy arrived.
The place of refuge for the weak old beggar,
A solitary mountain retreat, is good.

This also was composed by Kälden Gyatso.

རྒྱལ་མཚན་ཏོག་གི་ནོར་བུ་ལྟར།།
གང་འདོད་རེ་བ་སྐོང་མཛད་པའི།།
དྲིན་ཅན་བླ་མ་རིན་པོ་ཆེ།།
ཅི་བསམ་འགྲུབ་པའི་དངོས་གྲུབ་སྩོལ།།

ཀླུ་བློན་ཆེན་པོ་གནས་པའི་མཚོ།།
མཚོ་སྔོན་ཞེས་བྱའི་དབུས་ཀྱི་རི།།
རི་བོ་མ་ཧཱ་དེ་ཝའི་གནས།།
གནས་ཆེན་དེ་རུ་ཀླུ་འདི་བླངས།།

སེང་གེའི་ཕྲུ་གུ་དཀར་མོ་ཁྱོད།།
ཆུང་དུའི་དུས་ནས་གངས་ལ་དགའ།།
རྒྱུན་དུ་གངས་སྟོད་འཛིན་ཐུབ་ན།།
ངོ་མཚར་གཡུ་རལ་མགོ་ལ་རྒྱས།།

རྒྱ་སྟག་ཕྲུ་གུ་ཁྲ་བོ་ཁྱོད།།
ཆུང་ནས་ཙན་དན་ནགས་ལ་དགའ།།
རྒྱུན་དུ་ནགས་སྟོད་འཛིན་ཐུབ་ན།།
ངོ་མཚར་ཁྲ་འཛུམ་ལུས་ལ་བཀྲ།།

Precious, kind lama
Who fulfills my desires and hopes
Like a jewel on top of a victory banner—
Please grant me the *siddhi*s to accomplish whatever I intend.

As for the lake where the great minister of the *nāgas* dwells,
So-called Tsho Ngön,
In the middle of it is a mountain, the residence of Mahādeva.
At that sacred place I am singing this song.

You, a lion's white cub,
Have rejoiced in the snow mountain from an early age.
When you can always keep to the summit of the mountain,
A turquoise mane will grow on your head.

You, a tiger's multi-colored cub,
Have taken delight in the sandalwood forest since you were small.
When you can always grasp the treetops in the forest,
Your stripes will be vivid.

ཉ་མོའི་ཕྲུ་གུ་གསེར་མིག་ཁྱོད།།
ཆུང་ནས་རྒྱ་མཚོའི་ནང་ལ་དགའ།།
རྒྱུན་དུ་མཚོ་དཀྱིལ་འཛིན་ནུས་ན།།
ངོ་མཚར་གསེར་མིག་ལུས་ལ་འཁྱིལ།།

བླ་མ་དམ་པའི་སྲས་པོ་ཁྱོད།།
ཆུང་ནས་དབེན་པའི་རི་ལ་དགའ།།
རྒྱུན་དུ་རི་ཁྲོད་བསྟེན་ནུས་ན།།
ངོ་མཚར་ཉམས་རྟོགས་ཡོན་ཏན་སྐྱེ།།

མི་མེད་ལུང་སྟོང་རྒྱལ་བའི་ཞིང་།།
རང་ཉིད་གཅིག་པུ་རྒྱལ་བའི་སྲས།།
དཀའ་ཐུབ་ཏིང་འཛིན་མཛད་མེད་ཟས།།

ཨ་ཤད་གཏུམ་མོ་འཛད་མེད་གོས།།
འདི་འདྲ་བསྟེན་ན་ངོ་མཚར་ཆེ།།
འདི་རྣམས་རྒྱུན་དུ་བསྟེན་ནུས་ཤོག།

ཅེས་པ་འདི་ཡང་ཚོགས་དྲུག་རང་གྲོལ་ཤིན་ཏུ་སྐྱིད་པའི་ཤུགས་ཀྱིས་གླུ་རུ་བླངས་པའོ།།

You, a fish's golden-eyed fry,
Have been happy in the ocean from youth.
When you can always keep to the middle of the ocean,
The light of your golden eyes will shimmer.

You, the disciple of a holy teacher,
Have found joy in solitary mountains since you were small.
When you can always stay in a mountain hermitage,
Wondrous qualities of profound experience and realization will arise.

In the uninhabited empty valleys,
The Pure Realms of the Victorious Ones,
I myself, alone, the son of the Victorious Ones,
Have fed on the unfabricated *samādhi,* difficult to attain.

Clothed like this in the inexhaustible inner heat,
What wonder will arise!
On these clothes may you always be able to rely.

Tshogdruk Rangdrol sang this also, in a state of great happiness.

གནས་དབེན་པའི་དགའ་ཚལ་ཉམས་དགའ་རུ།།
ཆོས་བཤད་སྒྲུབ་ཐུབ་བསྟན་རྒྱལ་མཚན་དེ།།
འབད་བརྩོན་པའི་ཕྲུག་གིས་བསྒྲེངས་མཛད་པའི།།
ཁོང་མཁས་གྲུབ་ཡོངས་ཀྱི་ཞབས་ལ་འདུད།།

ཡུལ་ཕ་ཡུལ་བདུད་ཀྱི་བཙོན་ཁང་ན།།
གཏི་མུག་གི་མུན་པ་རབ་ཏུ་ནག།
འདོད་ཆགས་ཀྱི་མི་གཙང་འདམ་རྫབ་ཆེ།།
ཞེ་སྡང་གི་དུག་ཚེར་ཤིན་ཏུ་རྩུབ།།

གྲོགས་ཆུང་མའི་བཙོན་སྲུང་སྙིང་རྗེ་མེད།།
གཏན་ཆགས་སྡང་དགྲ་སྐད་རྒྱུན་ཆད་མེད།།
སྡུག་བསྔལ་གྱི་ཆད་པ་བཟོད་གླགས་མེད།།
སེམས་ནམ་ཡང་བདེ་བའི་གོ་སྐབས་མེད།།

སྔོན་བྱོན་པའི་མི་ལ་ཡབ་སྲས་དང་།།
ཡུལ་རེབ་གོང་མུན་སེལ་སྐལ་ལྡན་བཞིན།།
ད་མ་འདུག་མ་འདུག་མྱུར་དུ་བྲོས།།
ཡུལ་ཕ་ཡུལ་བཙོན་ར་རྒྱབ་ཏུ་ཞོག།
བཙོན་བསྲུང་གི་བུ་མོར་ལྟག་པ་སྟོན།།
གནས་དབེན་པའི་དགའ་ཚལ་ཉམས་དགར་བྲོས།།

I bow at the feet of all scholars and siddhas
Who with their own hands
Persevered in raising the victory banner of the Buddha's teachings,
Expounding and practicing the Dharma in pleasant groves
  of solitary places.

In the prison of the demonic forces, my homeland,
The obscuration of delusion is very black.
The impure and foulest swamp of lust is huge.
The poisonous thorns of anger are very sharp.

The jailers have no compassion for their friends and spouses,
Reciting the same old never-ending stories of love and hate.
The punishment of suffering is unbearable.
I never had a chance of being happy there.

Like those who came before, Milarepa and his disciples,
And Kälden, who dispelled the darkness in Rebgong,
Don't stay, don't stay, quickly proceed.
Place the prison of your homeland behind you.
Show the nape of your neck to the daughters of the prison guards.
Hasten to a pleasing grove of a hermitage.

སྔོན་རྒྱལ་བས་བྱང་ཆུབ་བརྙེས་པའི་ས།།
ཁོང་མཁས་གྲུབ་མང་པོ་བཞུགས་པའི་ཤུལ།།
ཡ་མཚན་པའི་དབེན་པའི་རི་ངོགས་ན།།
ངོ་མཚར་བའི་ལྟད་མོ་སྣ་ཚོགས་ཡོད།།

ཡར་སྐྱེད་ན་ལྷོ་སྤྲིན་ལང་མ་ཡིང་།།
མར་འོག་ན་ཆུ་གཙང་གྲུ་མ་གྲུ།།
བར་ཐང་ན་རྩི་ཤིང་བན་མ་བུན།།
བྱ་སྣ་ཚོགས་སྐད་སྙན་ཀྱུ་རུ་རུ།།
རྐང་དྲུག་ལྡན་གླུ་ལེན་དི་རི་རི།།
བྱ་རྒོད་པོའི་གཤོག་རྩལ་སྒྲོ་རོ་རོ།།
ཤ་རི་དྭགས་མང་པོ་ཤ་ར་ར།།

དེ་ལྟ་བུའི་གནས་སུ་ཕྱིན་པ་ན།།
ཁྱིམ་བཟའ་ཚང་སྐྱོང་རྒྱུ་མེད་པས་བདེ།།
ཁ་མི་སོས་དོགས་པ་མེད་པས་བདེ།།
རྒྱབ་མི་ཁེབས་སེམས་ཁུར་མེད་པས་བདེ།།
ཚོང་སོ་ནམ་རེམ་པོ་མི་དགོས་བདེ།།
ནོར་འཚོ་སྐྱོང་སྡུག་བསྔལ་མེད་པས་བདེ།།

On an amazing, solitary mountainside,
A place where the former Victorious Ones attained enlightenment,
A deserted place where many scholars and practitioners have dwelt,
There are such marvelous displays to behold.

Up above, southern clouds drift about gently,
Down below, streams meander,
And in between, fruit trees shimmer on the plain.
Birds chirp out with pleasing voices.
Creatures with six legs buzz, singing songs.
Vultures glide around on skillful wings.
Deer and other hoofed animals race along.

When I go to a place like that
Because there is no reason to take care of a family, I am happy.
Because there is no anxiety over not being able to feed others,
  I am happy.
Because there are no concerns about not covering people's backs,
  I am happy.
Because there is no need to strive at business or fieldwork,
  I am happy.
Because there is no suffering related to wealth and livelihood,
  I am happy.

ཡར་སོང་ན་གཅན་གཟོན་མེད་པས་བདེ།།
དགྲ་ནག་པོའི་འཐབ་རྩོད་མི་དགོས་བདེ།།
ཆོས་ཅི་བྱེད་རང་དབང་ཐོབ་པས་བདེ།།
དུས་གཏན་གྱི་འདུན་མ་འགྲུབ་པས་བདེ།།

ཚེ་འདི་དང་ཕྱི་མ་གཉིས་ཀ་བདེ།།
དུས་འདི་ནས་བཟུང་སྐྱེ་བདེ་བར་འགྲོ།།

ང་མ་འདུག་མ་འདུག་ད་ལྷ་གྲོས།།
ཁ་ཕྱི་ལ་མ་འཁོར་དབེན་པར་གྲོས།།
མིག་ཕྱི་ལ་མ་ལྟ་དབེན་པར་གྲོས།།
མིའི་གཏམ་ལ་མ་ཉན་དབེན་པར་གྲོས།།
ཅང་མ་བཤད་ཁ་རོག་དབེན་པར་གྲོས།།
བྱ་རྒོད་པོ་རྟི་ལས་ཐར་བཞིན་གྲོས།།
མི་ནག་ཅན་བཙོན་ནས་འབྲོས་བཞིན་གྲོས།།
ལར་བསམ་བློ་གང་ཡང་མ་གཏོང་གྲོས།།

Because there is no yoke pressing down on my neck from above,
I am happy.
Because I don't need to quarrel with enemies who have dark
thoughts and feelings, I am happy.
Because I have obtained the independence to do any Dharma
practices I wish, I am happy.
Because I am fulfilling my ultimate objectives, I am happy.

I will be happy in this and future lives..
From now on, I will go towards peace.

Now don't stay, don't stay, quickly proceed.
Don't turn your face back. Hasten to a solitary place.
Don't look back. Hasten to a solitary place.
Don't listen to other people. Hasten to a solitary place.
Don't explain anything whatsoever. Be silent. Hasten to a
solitary place.
Like a vulture escaping from a net, go on.
Like criminals fleeing from prison, go on.
In general, don't think about anything at all. Go on.

མར་འཁོར་བའི་བཙོན་རར་ཆུད་པའི་མི།།
གླུ་རབ་སྙན་སྟོབས་ལྡན་རྒྱལ་པོ་འདིས།།
ཡར་དབེན་པའི་ས་རུ་བཏང་ནས་ཀྱང་།།
ཆོས་ཉམས་ལེན་དགའ་བྲོ་འཁྲབ་པར་ཤོག།

ཅེས་པ་འདི་ཡང་འཁོར་བའི་བཙོན་ཁང་ན་རྒྱུན་དུ་ཉལ་ནས་ཆགས་སྡང་གི་སྨྲེ་སྔགས་འདོན་པའི་མི་རྣམས་དབེན་པའི་ས་རུ་གཏོང་ཨེ་ཐུབ་སྙམ་ནས། གླུ་དབྱངས་ཀྱི་མི་ཆེན་འདི་ཚོགས་དྲུག་རང་གྲོལ་གྱིས་མངགས་པའོ།།

May this rousing song, a powerful king,

Release those locked in the prison of samsara down below

Into a solitary place up above,

Where they may practice the Dharma and dance with joy!

Wondering whether people who lament over attraction and aversion, having slept continually in the prisons of samsara, could be released to a solitary place, chief singer Tshogdruk Rangdrol issued these commands.

Chapter Eleven

Meditation Experiences

ཕ་རྒན་ཆོས་རྒྱལ་དག་གི་དབང་བོའི་ཞབས་ལ་འདུད༎

ཚེ་འདིའི་བྱ་བ་ཐམས་ཅད་བློ་ཡིས་བཏང་ན་བཟང་༎
བློ་ཡིས་བཏང་ནས་རི་ཁྲོད་དབེན་པ་བསྟེན་ན་བཟང་༎
བསྟེན་ནས་བླ་མའི་གདམས་ངག་ཉམས་སུ་བླངས་ན་བཟང་༎
གདམས་པའི་ནང་ནས་རང་སེམས་སྟོང་གསལ་བསྒོམས་ན་བཟང་༎
སྒོམ་དུས་མི་གཡོ་རྩེ་གཅིག་ཉམས་པར་བཞག་ན་བཟང་༎
མཉམ་པར་བཞག་ནས་རྟོག་མེད་ངང་ལ་གནས་ན་བཟང་༎
ངང་ལ་གནས་པའི་མཉམ་གཞག་མཐའ་རུ་ཕྱིན་ན་བཟང་༎

བཟང་པོ་བདུན་གྱི་གླུ་འདི་ཚོགས་དྲུག་རང་གྲོལ་བླངས༎
ཐོས་ཚད་སྐྱ་སེར་ཕོ་མོའི་སེམས་ལ་ཕན་པར་ཤོག༎

I bow at the feet of the elderly father, Chögyäl Ngakyi Wangpo.

If one renounces all activities of this life, it is good.
Having renounced them, if one stays in a mountain hermitage,
  it is good.
Having stayed there, if one practices the lama's oral instructions,
  it is good.
Practicing the instructions, if one meditates on the emptiness
  and luminosity of one's own mind, it is good.
While meditating, if one settles without wavering, one-pointedly
  in equipoise, it is good.
Having settled in equipoise, if one abides in the state free of thoughts,
  it is good.
If the equipoise which abides in that state reaches perfection, it is good.

Tshogdruk Rangdrol sang this song of the seven goodnesses.
May it benefit the minds of all who heard it, monks and
  laypersons, men and women.

ཐུགས་མཁའ་ལྟར་སྟོང་ཞིང་རབ་ཏུ་ཡངས།།
ཕ་མ་ལྟར་དྲིན་ཆེ་ཆོས་རྒྱལ་ཕང་།།
མགོའི་ཞྭ་ལྟར་སྤྱི་བོའི་རྒྱན་དུ་བཞུགས།།
བུས་དྲན་ལྟར་འདུད་དོ་བྱིན་གྱིས་རློབས།།

རྗེ་མི་ལ་སྐལ་ལྡན་རྒྱ་མཚོ་སོགས།།
རྗེ་གོང་མའི་རྣམ་ཐར་རྗེས་ཞུགས་ནས།།
རྗེ་སྨ་ཆེན་བཞུགས་གནས་གངས་རི་ནས།།
རྗེ་ཆོས་རྒྱལ་བུ་དངས་གླུ་ཆུང་ལེན།།

ཁྱོད་ནམ་མཁའ་ཡངས་པར་དཔེ་ཞོག་ལ།།
སེམས་མཐའ་དབུས་མེད་པའི་སྒོམ་ཞིག་རྒྱོབ།།
ནང་རྣམ་རྟོག་ལྷོ་སྤྲིན་ལྟར་འཁྲིགས་ཀྱང་།།
སེམས་ནམ་མཁའ་བཞིན་དུ་བདེ་མོར་བཞུགས།།

ཁྱོད་འོད་གསལ་ཉི་མར་དཔེ་ཞོག་ལ།།
སེམས་གསལ་འགྲིབ་མེད་པའི་སྒོམ་ཞིག་རྒྱོབ།།
ནང་རྣམ་རྟོག་ཉི་ཟེར་ལྟར་འགྲོ་ཡང་།།
སེམས་ཉིམ་བཞིན་དུ་བདེ་མོར་བཞུགས།།

Your mind, like the sky, is empty and vast,
And your kindness, like that of parents, is great.
Chögyäl Wang—please be the crown that ornaments my head.
Thinking of you, I, your spiritual son, bow down. Please bless me.

Following the examples of the lords of former times,
Milarepa, Kälden Gyatso, and others,
I, a son of the lord Chögyäl, am singing a little song
On the snow-covered mountain, the dwelling place of
the lord of Machen.

Be inspired by the wide open sky.
Mind without center or edge—Meditate on that!
Though inner thoughts build up like southern clouds,
Mind, like the sky, is at ease.

Be inspired by the luminous sun.
Mind without shadow or light—Meditate on that!
Though inner thoughts radiate like beams,
Mind, like the sun, is at ease.

ཁྱོད་རྨ་ཆེན་རི་ལ་དགེ་ཞོག་ལ།།
སེམས་གཡོ་འགྱུལ་མེད་པའི་སྒོམ་ཞིག་སྒྲུབ།།
ནང་རྣམ་རྟོག་རྩི་ཤིང་ལྟར་སྐྱེ་ཡང་།།
སེམས་རི་བོ་བཞིན་དུ་བདེ་མོར་བཞུགས།།

ཁྱོད་རྒྱ་མཚོ་ཆེན་པོར་དགེ་ཞོག་ལ།།
སེམས་ཁ་གཏིང་མེད་པའི་སྒོམ་ཞིག་སྒྲུབ།།
ནང་རྣམ་རྟོག་ཆ་རླབས་ལྟར་འཁྲུགས་ཀྱང་།།
སེམས་རྒྱ་མཚོ་བཞིན་དུ་བདེ་མོར་བཞུགས།།

གླུ་སྟོན་ཆད་མང་པོ་མང་པོ་བླངས།།
གླུ་ལེན་ལ་ཤིན་ཏུ་ཤིན་ཏུ་དགའ།།
གླུ་འདི་ཡང་ལྟང་དེ་ལྟང་དེ་བླངས།།
གླུ་ཕོས་ཚད་ཧེ་སྐྱིད་ཧེ་སྐྱིད་ཤོག།

ཅེས་པ་འདི་རྣམས་ཀྱང་ཚོགས་དྲུག་རང་གྲོལ་གྱིས་བླངས་པའོ།།

Be inspired by Mount Machen.

Mind without tremor or quake—Meditate on that!

Though inner thoughts spread like thickets,

Mind, like the mountain, is at ease.

Be inspired by the vast, unbounded ocean.

Mind without surface or depth—Meditate on that!

Though inner thoughts roil like waves,

Mind, like the ocean, is at ease.

In former times, I sang many, many songs.

Singing songs, I felt such joy! Such joy!

Also I sung this song clearly, clearly!

May anyone who hears this song be happier and happier.

Tshogdruk Rangdrol also sang this.

ནམ་མཁའ་ལྟར།།
ཐུགས་ཡངས་པའི།།
ཀུ་རུ་མཁྱེན།།
ཆོས་དབྱིངས་ཀྱི།།
ཐང་ཆེན་ནས།།
རིག་སྟོང་གི།
རྟ་མཆོག་ཁ།།
གློད་ལ་ཐོངས།།
རྒྱུགས་རྒྱུགས་རྒྱུགས།།
ཡན་པར་རྒྱུགས།།
དགའ་ཡལ་ལེ།།
སྐྱིད་ཆིལ་ལེ།།
བན་མ་བྱུན།།
ཕྲུ་མ་འཕྲོ།།
འལ་མ་འོལ།།
ཤག་མ་ཤིག།
ཁྲལ་མ་ཁྲོལ།།
སངས་མ་སངས།།
ཡ་ལ་ལ།།

The guru
With a mind
As vast as the sky
Knows:

On the large plain
Of the *dharmadhātu*
Loosen the bit in the mouth
Of the superior horse
Of awareness and emptiness.
Let him go.
Gallop, gallop, gallop.
Gallop unrestrained.

Living joyfully...
Living happily...
Insubstantial as mist...
Floating...
Elusive...
Freely traveling...
Freely pervading...

ཡེངས་ཡེངས་ཡེངས།།

ཡེ་རེ་རེ།།

ཕྲུམ་ཕྲུམ་ཕྲུམ།།

མེ་རེ་རེ།།

གྲོལ་གྲོལ་གྲོལ།།

མ་ཡེངས་པའི།།

ལྷུག་གིས་གྲོལ།།

ཨ་ཡོ་ཤེ།

ཨེ་ཧ་ཧ།།

དེ་ཙམ་གྱིས།།

ཚོག་ནི་གྱིས།།

བན་རྒན་འབབ།།

གཡང་ཟློག་པོ།།

སེམས་བསྐྱེད་ཀྱི།།

ཤི་ཁར་བྱུང་།།

ཚོགས་བསགས་ཀྱི།།

ཛྭ་ཆུ་ཐུངས།།

ངོ་མཚར་ཆེ།།

ཨེ་མ་ཧོ།།

ཞེས་པ་འདི་ཡང་སྣང་བ་བན་བླུན་གྱི་ངང་ནས་སླུས་པའོ།།

Flashing...
Wandering...
Sham, sham, shammm...
Shimmering...

Urge, urge, urge,
Urge him on
With the crop of non-distraction.
A yo she!
E ha ha!

Make that much suffice.
The old monk dismounts.
"Great horse!"

He turns back to the mountain
Of *bodhicitta.*
He eats the herbs and drinks the water
Of gathered accumulations.
How wondrous!
E ma ho.

This also was expressed in a state of perceiving appearances to be as insubstantial as mist.

ཐོག་མའི་མགོན་ཀུན་བཟང་།།
མི་གཟུགས་སུ་ཤར་བའི།།
མཚན་ལྡན་གྱི་བླ་མ།།
ཆོས་རྒྱལ་ལ་འདུད་དོ།།

རང་རིག་ནི་འགྱུར་མེད།།
ནམ་མཁའ་ཡི་དབྱིངས་བཞིན།།
མཐའ་དབུས་ནི་མེད་པར།།
ཁྱབ་གདལ་དུ་འདུག་གོ།

གང་སྣང་གི་ཆོས་རྣམས།།
བར་སྣང་གི་འཇའ་བཞིན།།
སྣང་སྟོང་གི་གཟིགས་མོར།།
ལམ་ལམ་དུ་ཤར་བྱུང་།།

རྣམ་རྟོག་ཀུན་ཆུ་ལས།།
ཆུ་བུར་ནི་རྡོལ་བཞིན།།
ཤར་བ་དང་གྲོལ་བ།།
དུས་མཉམ་དུ་བུད་ཐལ།།

I bow to Chökyi Gyälpo—
The primordial lord Samantabhadra
Who has appeared in a human body
As a qualified master.

As for awareness that is aware of itself,
It does not change.
It is all-encompassing, without limits or center,
Like the wide open sky.

Manifestations of phenomena
Come forth vividly,
But the displays are empty,
Like rainbows in the sky.

All discursive thoughts
Appear, loosen,
And disappear simultaneously,
Like bubbles bursting forth from water.

ཆོས་དབྱིངས་ཀྱི་ཐང་ནས།།
འཁོར་འདས་ཀྱི་ལྟད་མོ།།
སྣ་ཚོགས་པ་མཐོང་བས།།
ངོ་མཚར་ཞིག་སྐྱེས་སོ།།

ཆོས་འཁོར་དབུས་པདྨའི།།
དགའ་ཚལ་གྱི་རང་སེམས།།
བྱུང་བ་པོ་ཉམས་རྟོགས།།
སྒྲུང་རྫུའི་རོས་སྒྲོས་ནས།།
ལྷ་མགུར་གྱི་སྒྲ་དབྱངས།།
སྙན་མོ་འདི་བླངས་སོ།།
དགེ་བ་ཡིས་འགྲོ་ཀུན།།
འབད་མེད་དུ་གྲོལ་ཤོག།

ཅེས་པ་འདི་ཡང་རེབ་གོང་གླུ་བ་ཚོགས་དྲུག་རང་གྲོལ་གྱིས་བླངས་པའོ།།

Since I have seen many displays
Of cyclical existence and its transcendence
On the plain of the *dharmadhātu,*
Wonder has arisen in me.

In the center of the heart *cakra*
Grows a lotus grove where the bee of my own mind
Has become intoxicated with the honey
Of profound experiences and realization.

I have sung
This melodious, pleasing song of the view.
Through this merit,
May all beings be liberated effortlessly.

The singer of Rebgong, Tshogdruk Rangdrol, sang this also.

ཨེ་མ་ཉམས་དགའ་རིག་པ་དྭངས།།

འདུ་འཛི་མེད་པའི་དབེན་གནས་སུ།།
རང་བྱུང་བྲག་གི་ཕུག་པ་རུ།།
སྒོ་ལྷོང་རྩྭ་དང་འབོལ་གདན་ལ།།
གཅིག་པུར་དྲང་སྲོང་སྤྱོད་ཚུལ་གྱིས།།
གནས་ནས་བྱམས་དང་སྙིང་རྗེ་དང་།།
བྱང་ཆུབ་སེམས་ཀྱིས་ཀུན་བསླངས་ནས།།
ལུས་བསྲུངས་ངག་གི་བཟླ་བ་སྤངས།།

རྣམ་རྟོག་སྤྲིན་ཕུང་དྭངས་སུ་བཅུག།
སེམས་ཀྱི་ནམ་མཁའ་ཧྲིག་གེར་བལྟ།།
ཉམས་ཀྱི་འཇའ་ཚོན་ཅི་ཤར་ཡང་།།
དེ་ལ་ཆེད་འཛིན་མེད་པར་བཞག།

བསྒོམ་རྒྱུ་རྡུལ་ཙམ་མི་དམིགས་ཀྱང་།།
ཡེངས་སུ་སྐད་ཅིག་ཙམ་ཡང་མེད།།

དེ་ལྟར་མཉམ་པར་བཞག་ཙ་ན།།
བཞག་དུས་མི་གཡོ་རི་དབང་བཞིན།།
ཅི་ཙམ་བཞག་པ་དེ་ཙམ་གནས།།

E ma! Joyous, clear awareness!

Yogis live in natural caves
In solitary places with no clamor,
Practicing alone like the Indian sages
On green grass and mats.
Arousing the wish to have love, compassion and *bodhicitta,*
They straighten their bodies and abandon all speech.

Clouds of thoughts clear.
They see the sky of mind vividly.
Though rainbows of feelings appear,
They do not fixate upon them.

Although they do not focus
On the slightest trace of a meditation object,
They are not distracted for an instant.

When they place their minds in equipoise like that,
Mind does not move, like Meru, lord of mountains.
The more their minds settle, the more they come to rest.

བཏང་ན་དགེ་བའི་དམིགས་པ་གང་།།
ཡིན་ཡང་ཐོགས་པ་མེད་པར་འཇུག།
ལུས་སེམས་ལས་རུང་བདེ་ཆེན་འདྲེན།།

མ་བསྒྲུབས་ལྷ་ཞལ་མང་པོ་མཐོང་།།
མངོན་ཤེས་རྫུ་འཕྲུལ་ཅིར་ཡང་འབྱུང་།།

དེ་ཡི་གྲགས་པ་ཟླ་འོད་ཀྱིས།།
ལྷ་མིའི་རྨོངས་པའི་མུན་པ་སེལ།།
ལག་པའི་པདྨོ་དབང་མེད་བསྐུམས།།
རབ་ཏུ་གུས་པས་ཕྱག་འཚལ་ཞིང་།།
མཁའ་ལས་ལྷ་ཡི་རོལ་མོ་བརྡུངས།།
བདུག་སྤོས་མེ་ཏོག་ཆར་བ་འབེབས།།
ས་ནས་མི་ཡིས་ཟས་གོས་འབུལ།།
ཡ་མཚན་གཏམ་སྙན་ཕྱོགས་བཅུར་སྒྲོག།

བསྟན་དང་འགྲོ་བ་མ་ལུས་ལ།།
དངོས་སམ་བརྒྱུད་ནས་ཕན་ཐོགས་པའི།།
དེ་འདྲའི་སྒོམ་ཆེན་པ་ཞིག་གྱིས།།

When yogis let go,
Though their minds fill with virtuous thoughts,
There are no obstructions.
Their bodies and minds are still competent,
But they are drawn into great bliss.

Yogis can see faces of deities naturally.
Miraculous displays of supernatural perceptions appear everywhere.

The moonlight of the yogis' renown
Clears away the darkness of delusion of deities and humans.
The lotuses of their disciples' hands close by themselves.
They prostrate themselves with respect
And divine music reverberates from the sky.
Rains of incense and flowers descend.
On the earth, people offer food and clothing.
They call out wondrous, gentle words in the ten directions.

Be a yogi like that
Who directly or indirectly benefits
The teachings and all beings without exception.

དེ་མིན་གྲོང་ལྷག་དགོན་ཆུང་དང་།།
རི་ཕུག་བྲག་ཕུག་འགའ་རེ་ན།།
བསྡད་རུང་སེམས་དེ་གྲོང་དུ་བཏང་།།

དགེ་སློང་བྱུས་རུང་འདུལ་ཁྲིམས་དང་།།
དགེ་སྦྱོང་ཆོས་བཞི་རྩ་ལྷུར་དོར།།

བྱ་བཏང་བྱུས་རུང་ཧམ་པ་ཆེ།།
ཟས་ནོར་ཁྱིམ་པ་ལས་ཀྱང་གསོག།

དེ་འདྲའི་སྒྲོམ་ཆེན་གཟུགས་བརྙན་གྱིས།།
ཅི་བྱ་དེ་བས་འཇིག་རྟེན་གྱིས།།

ཞེས་པ་འདི་ཡང་བདག་གི་ཡིད་ལ་ཤར་ཚེ་སློབ་བུ་ཡོངས་ལ་ཕན་ཕྱིར་དབེན་གནས་ཙཱ་རི་ནས་སྨྲས་པའོ།།

Otherwise, turn your back to the village,
Stay in a small monastery, or some mountain cave or rock cave,
And renounce your homeland.

Although you have made yourself a monk of the highest order,
Cast away the *Vinaya* rules of monastic discipline
And the four principles of virtuous training like grass,
If they are not important to you.

And if your vows are insincere,
Though you call yourself a renunciant, your greed will be great,
And you will accumulate even more food and wealth than
a householder.

Sustaining the facade of a yogi like that, what good will you do?
If you are not sincere in your practices, be a person of the world.

I spoke this as it came to mind, in order to benefit all the disciples at the hermitage in Tsari.

དཔེར་ན་རྟ་རྩལ་ཅན་གྱི་མིས།།
མདའ་དང་མེ་མདའ་རྒྱག་པ་སོགས།།
བྱ་བ་ཅི་བྱེད་རྟ་ཐོག་ནས།།
མ་བབས་བཞིན་དུ་བྱེད་པ་ལྟར།།
མཉམ་བཞག་ནམ་མཁའ་ལྟ་བུ་ལ།།
བརྟན་པ་ཐོབ་པའི་རྣལ་འབྱོར་པས།།
མཉམ་བཞག་དང་ལས་མ་གཡོས་བཞིན།།
མཁའ་ལ་འཇའ་ཚོན་འཐེན་པ་ལྟར།།
བློ་ཡི་ཟུར་གྱིས་བསྐྱེད་རྫོགས་སོགས།།
རྗེས་ཐོབ་སྒྱུ་མའི་སྤྱོད་པ་གྱིས།།

དཔེར་ན་རྟ་རྩལ་མེད་པའི་མིས།།
མདའ་དང་མེ་མདའ་རྒྱག་པ་སོགས།།
བྱ་བ་ཅི་བྱེད་རྟ་ཐོག་ནས།།
ས་ལ་བབས་ནས་བྱེད་པ་ལྟར།།
མཉམ་བཞག་ནམ་མཁའ་ལྟ་བུ་ལ།།
བརྟན་པ་མ་ཐོབ་རྣལ་འབྱོར་པས།།
མཉམ་བཞག་དང་ནས་ཚུར་ལངས་ནས།།
སྒྱུ་མ་མཁན་གྱི་སྤྲུལ་སྒྱུར་ལྟར།།
ཚོགས་བསགས་སྒྲིབ་སྦྱོང་ལས་སོགས་པ།།
རྗེས་ཐོབ་སྒྱུ་མའི་སྤྱོད་པ་གྱིས།།

Just as a skilled horseman
Does such things
As shooting arrows and guns
On horseback, without dismounting,
Likewise, a yogi who has attained stability in sky-like
meditative equipoise
Performs worldly activities without moving from his meditative state.
Accordingly, in between meditation sessions
Of Generation Stage, Completion Stage, and so on,
You should perform the practice of seeing things with a facet of
your mind as illusions,
Like rainbows drawn across the sky,

Just as a person unskilled with horses
Does such things
As shooting arrows and guns
After dismounting from his horse,
Likewise, a yogi who has not attained stability
In sky-like meditative equipoise
Arises from his meditations to perform worldly activities.
Accordingly, in between sessions of such deeds as
Gathering the accumulations and the purifying obscurations,
You should perform the practice of seeing things as illusions,
The conjurings of a magician.

བསོད་ནམས་ཚོགས་དང་ཡེ་ཤེས་ཚོགས།།
མཐར་ཐུག་སྐུ་གཉིས་ཐོབ་པའི་རྒྱུ།།
གནས་སྐབས་ཕན་ཚུན་གཅིག་གྲོགས་སུ།།
གཅིག་འགྱུར་གཅིག་བོགས་གཅིག་གིས་འདོན།།

དེ་ཕྱིར་བསོད་ནམས་ཡེ་ཤེས་ཚོགས།།
ཟུང་འབྲེལ་བྱེད་པ་བོགས་ཆེ་བས།།
མཉམ་བཞག་ནམ་མཁའ་ལྟ་བུ་ཡི།།
ཡེ་ཤེས་ཚོགས་ལ་འབད་པར་བྱ།།
མཉམ་པར་བཞག་ན་མི་འདོད་དུས།།
རྗེས་ཐོབ་སྒྱུ་མ་ལྟ་བུ་ཡི།།
བསོད་ནམས་ཚོགས་ལ་འབད་པར་བྱ།།
དེ་ལ་སྐྱོ་ནས་མི་འདོད་དུས།།
མཉམ་བཞག་ནམ་མཁའ་ལྟ་བུ་སྐྱོངས།།

དེ་ལྟར་རེ་མོས་བྱས་ཙ་ན།།
གནས་སྐབས་གཅིག་བོགས་གཅིག་གིས་འདོན།།
མཐར་ཐུག་སྐུ་གཉིས་ཐོབ་པར་འགྱུར།།

As for the accumulations of merit and wisdom,
The means for attaining the two ultimate bodies of a Buddha—
Each mutually helps the other
And a gain for one is a gain for the other.
The advantage of accumulating merit and wisdom
As a pair is great.

You should strive to accumulate the wisdom
Of sky-like meditative equipoise.
But when you do not want to rest in equipoise,
In between sessions you should exert yourself in accumulating merit,
Which is illusory.
And, having tired of that, when you no longer want to
accumulate merit,
Sustain your experience of meditative equipoise, like the sky.

In that way, by doing these acts in turn,
The accumulation of one incidentally benefits the accumulation
of the other,
And you will attain the two ultimate bodies of the Buddha.

Chapter Twelve

Happiness

ན་མོ་གུ་རུ།

དབྱར་གསུམ་ནམ་ཟླ་དེ་སླེབས་བྱུང་།།
རྒྱལ་ལྡན་གཡུ་འབྲུག་ངའི་སྐྱིད་པ།།
ལྷོ་སྤྲིན་སྨུག་པོ་དང་བསྡེབས་ནས།།
ལྷ་ལམ་ཡངས་པ་རུ་ཆས་འགྲོ།།

མེ་ཏོག་སྣ་ཚོགས་ནི་སྐྱེས་བྱུང་།།
ཡིད་འོང་བྱུང་བ་ངའི་སྐྱིད་པ།།
འདབ་མ་ལེགས་པོ་དེ་བརྒྱངས་ནས།།
གང་བཟང་མེ་ཏོག་སར་ཆས་འགྲོ།།

ཟླ་མས་གདམས་ངག་ནི་གནང་བྱུང་།།
སྐལ་ལྡན་བྱ་བཏང་ངའི་སྐྱིད་པ།།
གསལ་འདེབས་བཞུ་བུམ་དེ་ཁུར་ནས།།
དབེན་གནས་གང་བཟང་ལ་ཆས་འགྲོ།།

ཞེས་པ་འདི་ནི་ཚོགས་དྲུག་རང་གྲོལ་གྱིས་ཉམས་དགའི་གླུ་རུ་བླངས་པའོ།།

I bow to the guru.

The three months of summer have arrived.
I, a mighty, turquoise thunder-dragon, am happy.
The dark southern clouds have been gathering
And I set forth through the broad sky.

Many kinds of flowers have come up.
I, an enchanting bee, am happy.
The leaves have been unfolding
And I set forth across the land to find any good flowers.

A lama gave me his oral instructions.
I, a fortunate renunciant, am happy.
Carrying my manual of brief reminders,
I set forth for any good hermitage.

I, Tshogdruk Rangdrol, expressed my delight in this song.

ཕ་ཆོས་རྒྱལ་ངག་གི་དབང་པོར་འདུད།།
བུའི་ལུས་སེམས་བདེ་བར་བྱིན་གྱིས་རློབས།།

ཡུལ་ཕ་ཡུལ་སྐྱིད་ནས་ཞེ་སྡང་འབྱུང་།།
ངས་ད་ལྷ་རྒྱབ་ཏུ་སྤངས་པས་བདེ།།

གཉེན་ཉེ་འབྲེལ་སྐྱིད་ནས་གདུང་སེམས་འབྱུང་།།
ངས་ད་ལྷ་ལྷག་པ་བསྟན་པས་བདེ།།

རྒྱུ་ནོམ་པའི་སྐྱིད་ནས་སེར་སྣ་འབྱུང་།།
ངས་ད་ལྷ་གསོག་འཇོག་མ་བྱས་བདེ།།

ཟས་ཞིམ་མངར་སྐྱིད་ནས་འདོད་སྲེད་འབྱུང་།།
ངས་ད་ལྷ་ངན་ངོན་ཟོས་པས་བདེ།།

གྲོང་དགོན་སྡེའི་སྐྱིད་ནས་རྣམ་གཡེང་འབྱུང་།།
ངས་ད་ལྷ་རི་ཁྲོད་འགྲིམས་པས་བདེ།།

འཁོར་གྲྭ་སློབ་སྐྱིད་ནས་ཆགས་སྡང་འབྱུང་།།
ང་ད་ལྷ་གཅིག་པུར་བསྡད་པས་བདེ།།

I bow to the father, Chögyäl Ngakyi Wangpo.
Please bless me, your son, so that my body may be at ease and
my mind happy.

Relying on a homeland causes anger to arise.
Because I have now left mine behind, I am happy.

Relying on relatives causes misery to arise.
Because I have now shown them the nape of my neck, I am happy.

Relying on wealth causes greed to arise.
Because I no longer collect or hoard, I am happy.

Relying on delicious, sweet food causes cravings to arise.
Because I have now been eating just what I absolutely need, I am happy.

Relying on monastic communities in villages causes distractions to arise.
Because I have now been wandering among mountain hermitages,
I am happy.

Relying on entourages of monks and disciples causes jealousy to arise.
Because I have been living alone, I am happy.

ང་རྣལ་འབྱོར་བདེ་ཚུལ་གླུ་དབྱངས་འདི།།
གང་ཐོས་ཚད་བདེ་ཞིང་སྐྱིད་པར་ཤོག།

ཅེས་པ་འདི་ཡང་བདེ་ཞུས་ཞིག་གི་ལན་དུ་ཚོགས་དྲུག་རང་གྲོལ་གྱིས་གནས་ཆེན་ཁྲིད་འཕགས་མཚོ་སྙིང་ནས་སྨྲས་པའོ།།

As for this song about how a yogi achieves happiness,

May whoever hears it be happy and joyous.

I, Tshogdruk Rangdrol, said this at the sacred, especially noble place, Tshonying, when someone asked me how I was.

འདུལ་རྒྱུའི་དགྲ་ཡང་མེད་ལ།།
སྐྱོང་རྒྱུའི་གཉེན་ཡང་མེད་པར།།
ཕྱོགས་མེད་རི་ཁྲོད་འགྲིམ་པའི།།
ཆོས་པ་རྣམས་ཀྱི་སྐྱིད་ལ།།

ཕར་བལྟས་དཔོན་པོ་མེད་ལ།།
ཚུར་བལྟས་གཡོག་པོ་མེད་པར།།
ཕྱོགས་མེད་རི་ཁྲོད་འགྲིམ་པའི།།
ཆོས་པ་རྣམས་ཀྱི་སྐྱིད་ལ།།

གར་སོང་རྩད་གཅོད་མེད་ལ།།
འདིར་ཞོག་ཟེར་མི་མེད་པར།།
ཕྱོགས་མེད་རི་ཁྲོད་འགྲིམ་པའི།།
ཆོས་པ་རྣམས་ཀྱི་སྐྱིད་ལ།།

འདུག་ན་ལས་རྒྱུ་མེད་ལ།།
འགྲོ་ན་ལུས་རྒྱུ་མེད་པར།།
ཕྱོགས་མེད་རི་ཁྲོད་འགྲིམ་པའི།།
ཆོས་པ་རྣམས་ཀྱི་སྐྱིད་ལ།།

With no enemies at all to tame
And no relatives at all to care for,
Yogis who wander aimlessly
Among mountain hermitages are happy.

With no lords looking upon them from afar
And no servants looking at them from nearby,
Yogis who wander aimlessly
Among mountain hermitages are happy.

Without people seeking them out wherever they go,
And without people telling them to come back,
Yogis who wander aimlessly
Among mountain hermitages are happy.

When they stay, there is nothing to do,
And when they go, there is nothing to leave behind.
Yogis who wander aimlessly
Among mountain hermitages are happy.

གསལ་འདེབས་བེའུ་བུམ་ཞིག་ཁུར།།
སྦྲ་དབྱུག་ཕྱག་ཏུ་བསྣམས་ནས།།
ཕྱོགས་མེད་རི་ཁྲོད་འཁྲིམ་པའི།།
ཆོས་པ་རྣམས་ཀྱི་སྐྱིད་ལ།།

ཕྱག་བདར་ཁྲོད་ཀྱི་གོས་འཆང་།།
བཟའ་བཏུང་སློང་མོར་བརྟེན་ནས།།
ཕྱོགས་མེད་རི་ཁྲོད་འཁྲིམ་པའི།།
ཆོས་པ་རྣམས་ཀྱི་སྐྱིད་ལ།།

སླུག་པ་ཅན་གྱི་རི་ན།།
སྒོམ་ཐག་ཁོར་ཅིག་གྱོན་ཏེ།།
ཏིང་ངེ་འཛིན་ལ་ཞུགས་པའི།།
ཆོས་པ་རྣམས་ཀྱི་སྐྱིད་ལ།།

ན་ན་འདྲི་མི་མེད་ལ།།
ཤི་ན་ངུ་མི་མེད་པར།།
རི་དྭགས་ལྷ་བུར་འཆི་བའི།།
ཆོས་པ་རྣམས་ཀྱི་སྐྱིད་ལ།།

Carrying a manual of brief reminders,
And grasping a walking stick in their hands,
Yogis who wander aimlessly
Among mountain hermitages are happy.

Wearing clothes made from old rags,
And relying on alms for food and drink,
Yogis who wander aimlessly
Among mountain hermitages are happy.

Wearing a single strip of the meditation belt
In the misty mountains,
Yogis who have entered into *samādhi*
Are happy.

If they are sick, no one inquires about them,
And if they die, no one cries.
Yogis who die like deer
Are happy.

ཚེ་མཇུག་འདི་ལ་དེ་འདྲའི།།
སྐལ་བ་བདག་ལ་བྱུང་ན།།
ཚོགས་དྲུག་རང་གྲོལ་དགའ་བ།།
ཚོགས་དྲུག་རང་གྲོལ་སྐྱིད་པ།།

ཞེས་པ་འདི་ཡང་ཉིན་ཞིག་སེམས་ལ་ཤར་བ་ལྟར་བྲིས་པའོ།།

If fortune like that

Comes to me at the end of my life,

Tshogdruk Rangdrol will rejoice.

Tshogdruk Rangdrol will be happy.

I wrote this one day, according to whatever came to mind.

བདེ་ཆེན་ཆོས་དབྱིངས་ཕོ་བྲང་དུ།།
བདེ་བར་བཞུགས་པའི་བླ་མ་ལ།།
རབ་ཏུ་གུས་པས་ཕྱག་བྱས་ནས།།
རྣལ་འབྱོར་བདེ་ལུགས་དབྱངས་སུ་ལེན།།

བླ་མས་ངེས་དོན་བསྟན་ནས་བཟུང་།།
གུ་ཡངས་ཡན་པ་བློ་རི་བདེ།།

ཆོས་རྣམས་བར་སྣང་འཇའ་ཚོན་བཞིན།།
སེམས་ཀྱི་དབྱིངས་སུ་ཤར་བས་བདེ།།

སེམས་ཉིད་ནམ་མཁའ་ཡངས་པ་ལྟར།།
སྟོང་གསལ་མཐའ་དབུས་མེད་པས་བདེ།།

མཉམ་རྗེས་སྣང་སེམས་རོ་གཅིག་འདྲེས།།
ལྟད་མོ་ཅིར་ཡང་མཐོང་བས་བདེ།།

འཁོར་འདས་ཐམས་ཅད་སེམས་སུ་རྫོགས།།
སྲིད་ཞིའི་སྤྲང་བླང་བྲལ་བས་བདེ།།

བསྒོམ་བྱ་སྒོམ་བྱེད་གཅིག་ཏུ་འདྲེས།།
བསྒོམ་རྒྱུ་རྡུལ་ཙམ་མེད་པས་བདེ།།

Having prostrated myself with great respect
To the lama who dwells blissfully
In the palace of *dharmadhātu*, Sukhāvatī,
I will sing a melodious song about how a yogi achieves happiness.

The lama showed me true meaning, and I perceived it.
A vast , free mind is very happy.

Because phenomena arise in the space of my mind
Like rainbows in the sky, I am happy.

The nature of mind is empty and luminous, like the broad sky.
Because it has no center or edge, I am happy.

Meditation and post-meditation, and appearance and mind have
blended to one taste.
Because I look at any display of phenomena like this, I am happy.

All cyclic existence and transcendence are complete within mind.
Because I neither accept nor reject samsara or Nirvana, I am happy.

Objects of meditation and the meditator have blended together.
Because the aim of meditation is not mere discipline, I am happy.

མི་བསྒོམ་སྙམ་ཡང་སྒོམ་དུ་སོང་།།
བསྒོམ་ལ་རྒྱུན་འཆད་མེད་པས་བདེ།།

དེ་ལྟར་མ་རྟོགས་འགྲོ་བ་ལ།།
ཕྱོགས་མེད་སྙིང་རྗེ་སྐྱེས་པས་བདེ།།

སྒྱུ་མ་མཁན་གྱི་སྒྱུལ་སྒྱུར་ལྟར།།
ཞེན་མེད་འགྲོ་དོན་བྱས་པས་བདེ།།

ནམ་ཞིག་སྒྱུ་ལུས་འཇིག་པའི་ཚེ།།
འཆི་བ་ཆོས་སྐུར་གྲོལ་བས་བདེ།།

ཆོས་སྐུའི་དབྱིངས་ལས་མ་གཡོས་བཞིན།།
གཟུགས་སྐུས་འགྲོ་དོན་འོང་བས་བདེ།།

ཚེ་འདིར་བདེ་ཞིང་ཕྱི་མར་སྐྱིད།།
ཀུན་ཀྱང་འདི་ལྟར་བདེ་བར་སྨོན།།

ཞེས་པ་འདི་ཡང་དད་བརྩོན་ཤེས་རབ་སྙིང་རྗེ་དང་ལྡན་པའི་སློབ་བུ་སངས་རྒྱས་དོན་གྲུབ་ཀྱིས་བདེ་ཞུས་བྱས་པའི་སྐབས་སེམས་ལ་ཤར་བ་ལྟར་ཡི་གེར་བྲིས་པའོ།།

Although I thought I was not meditating, I am.
Because meditation neither continues nor ends, I am happy.

Because indiscriminate compassion for all unrealized beings
Has been born in me, I am happy.

Because I have acted for the benefit of beings without longing for things—
A magician's conjurings—I am happy.

Because whenever an illusory body perishes,
The one who dies is liberated into the *dharmakāya*, I am happy.

Because form bodies will come for the benefit of all beings
Without moving from the realm of the *dharmakāya*, I am happy.

In this life I am happy and in the next one I will be happy.
I pray that all beings also will be happy like this.

When Sangye Dondrub, a disciple with faith, diligence, wisdom, and compassion, asked me how I was, I wrote down whatever came to mind.

ཆོས་ཀྱི་རྒྱལ་པོར་གུས་པས་འདུད།།

ཨེ་མ་རྫོགས་ཆེན་རྣལ་འབྱོར་པ།།
བྱ་བཏང་ཚོགས་དྲུག་རང་གྲོལ་སེམས།།
ནམ་མཁའ་བཞིན་དུ་རྒྱ་རེ་ཆེ།།
ས་གཞི་བཞིན་དུ་སྲ་ཞིང་བརྟན།།
རྒྱ་མཚོ་བཞིན་དུ་དྭངས་ཤིང་གསལ།།

ཆོས་ཀུན་སེམས་ཀྱི་རྩལ་དུ་རྫོགས།།
འཁོར་འདས་གཉིས་ཀྱིས་འཛིན་པ་བདག།
བདག་གཞན་དགྲ་གཉེན་དགག་སྒྲུབ་བྲལ།།
ཆོས་དབྱིངས་དང་དུ་མེར་གྱིས་སོང་།།

གང་དུ་བསྡད་ཀྱང་ཉམས་རེ་དགའ།།
སུ་དང་འགྲོགས་ཀྱང་ཞེ་རེ་བྲོད།།
མི་དགའ་བྱ་བའི་མིང་ཡང་མེད།།
གུ་ཡངས་ཡན་པ་བློ་རེ་བདེ།།

ཆོས་དབྱིངས་དང་དུ་དགའ་ཡལ་ལེ།།
ཨེ་མ་རྨད་བྱུང་སྐལ་བ་བཟང་།།
འདི་ཐོས་རྒྱུད་ལ་ཕན་པར་ཤོག།

I bow respectfully to Chökyi Gyälpo.

E ma, as for the mind of the renunciant, Tshogdruk Rangdrol,
The yogi of *Dzogchen,*
It is very wide and vast like the sky.
It is solid and firm like the earth.
It is pure and clear, like the ocean.

All phenomena are exhausted as displays of the mind.
I, who am caught up in both cyclic existence and its transcendence,
Must be free of distinguishing between
Myself and others, friends and enemies, accepting and rejecting
And go forward fully into the realm of the *dharmadhātu!*

Wherever I live, I will be delighted.
Whomever I associate with, I will feel joyful.
There will not be even the slightest hint of unpleasantness.
My mind will be carefree, detached, and at ease.

In the realm of the *dharmadhātu,* I will glow with bliss.
E ma, my wondrous fortune will be good.
May benefit come to the mind-stream of those who heard this.

ན་མོ་གུ་རུ།།

སེང་གེ་གདངས་དཀར་ལྗོངས་ན་བདེ།།

ཀོང་པོ་བྲག་དམར་ཀླུང་ན་བདེ།།

རི་དྭགས་སྤྱང་གཞོངས་འཛམ་པོར་བདེ།།

ཉ་མོ་མཚོ་ཡི་ནང་ན་བདེ།།

སྟག་མོ་ནགས་ཀྱི་གསེབ་ན་བདེ།།

ང་རྣལ་འབྱོར་དབེན་པའི་རི་ན་བདེ།།

སྟེང་ན་སྲ་བའི་བྲག་ཁུང་བདེ།།

འོག་ན་སྤོ་ལྗང་རྩྭ་གདན་བདེ།།

བར་ན་རྣལ་འབྱོར་སྒྱུ་ལུས་བདེ།།

དག་ནས་ཀླུ་དབྱངས་བླངས་པས་བདེ།།

སེམས་ལ་ཉམས་རྟོགས་ཤར་བས་བདེ།།

ཡོན་བདག་འཁོར་བཅས་བདེ་ལེགས་སམ།།

ཞེས་པ་འདི་ཡང་བྲུ་བཏང་ཚོགས་དྲུག་རང་གྲོལ་གྱིས་ཨ་རིག་གི་དད་ཅན་
ཡོན་བདག་འགའ་ལ་རྗེ་མཚར་དུ་བླངས་པའོ།།

I prostrate myself to the guru.

A lion on the summit of a snow mountain is happy.
A vulture on top of a red rock is happy.
A deer in a soft green meadow is happy.
A female fish in a lake is happy.
A tiger in the midst of a forest is happy.
I, a yogi in a mountain hermitage, am happy.
Above is a solid cave—happy.
Below is a green grass mat—happy.
In between, the illusory body of a yogi is happy.
Since I have sung songs with my voice, I am happy.
Since profound experience and realization have arisen
in my mind, I am happy.

Patrons with a retinue, are you happy?

The renunciant Tshogdruk Rangdrol sang this playfully to several faithful patrons of Arig.

Chapter Thirteen

Singing

ན་མོ་གུ་རུ།

རྒྱལ་གསུམ་རྫོགས་པའི་གཡུ་འབྲུག།
དབྱར་གསུམ་ནམ་མཁར་འཁྱོ་དུས།།
གསུང་སྙན་དར་དིར་སྒྲོགས་དང་།།
རྨ་བྱའི་སེམས་ལ་ཕན་ནོ།།

ལང་ཚོ་གསར་བའི་ལྷོ་སྤྲིན།།
མཁའ་ལ་ཡང་ཡོང་འཁྲིགས་དུས།།
སྦྲང་ཆར་འཇམ་པོ་ཕོབས་དང་།།
ཁུ་བྱུག་སེམས་ལ་ཕན་ནོ།།

བྱ་བཏང་ཚོགས་དྲུག་རང་གྲོལ།།
ཕྱོགས་མེད་རི་ཁྲོད་འགྲིམ་དུས།།
མགུར་དབྱངས་ལྷང་ལྷང་འཐེན་དང་།།
དད་ཅན་སེམས་ལ་ཕན་ནོ།།

ཞེས་པ་འདི་ནི་རང་ལ་སྨྲས་པའོ།།

I bow to the guru.

When you, the turquoise thunder-dragon who has
perfected the three skills,
Soar in the summer sky,
Call out with a pleasing, loud, rumbling voice!
It will inspire the peacocks.

When you, fresh, southern clouds
Gather and gently drift about the sky,
Cause a gentle rain to fall!
It will inspire the cuckoos.

When you, the renunciant Tshogdruk Rangdrol,
Wander aimlessly among mountain hermitages,
Sing *gur* melodies clearly!
It will inspire the faithful.

I said this to myself.

སྙིང་ནས་རྩ་བརྒྱུད་བླ་མའི།།
བྱིན་རླབས་སྤྲིན་ལྟར་གཏིབས་བྱུང་།།

བར་ན་ཡི་དམ་ལྷ་ཡིས།།
དངོས་གྲུབ་ཆར་བཞིན་ཕབ་བྱུང་།།

དེ་འོག་ཆོས་སྐྱོང་སྲུང་མས།།
འཕྲིན་ལས་གློག་ལྟར་འཁྱུག་བྱུང་།།

མདུན་ནས་རྡོ་རྗེ་སྤྲིན་ཚོས།།
གླུ་དབྱངས་འབྲུག་བཞིན་ལྡིར་བྱུང་།།

སྣོད་རྣམས་གཞལ་ཡས་ཁང་དང་།།
བཅུད་རྣམས་ལྷ་དང་ལྷ་མོ།།
རང་སྣང་དག་པ་དོན་གྱི།།
འོག་མིན་གནས་མཆོག་འདི་རུ།།
ལྷ་དང་ཌཱ་ཀི་མཉེས་ཕྱིར།།
སྙན་པའི་གླུ་དབྱངས་ལེན་ནོ།།
དགའ་བའི་གར་སྟབས་བསྒྱུར་རོ།།
སྐྱིད་པའི་ཀང་བྲོ་བྱེད་དོ།།

Above, my root and lineage lamas' blessings
Have gathered like clouds.

In between, *yidam* deities
Have caused the *siddhi*s to fall like rain.

Below that, protectors and guardians of the Dharma
Dart around like lightning, performing deeds.

In front, *vajra* brothers
Are roaring like thunder, singing songs.

In order that the deities and *ḍākinīs* take delight
In this ultimately supreme place, Akaniṣṭha,
With its pure, self-arising manifestations—
Celestial palaces
And their inhabitants, male and female deities—
We are singing a lovely song.
We are turning, with happy dance steps.
We are performing joyful dances.

ན་མོ་གུ་རུ།

དགའ་ལྡན་ལྷ་ཡི་ཡུལ་གྱི།།
ངོ་མཚར་སྐྱེད་མོས་ཚལ་ན།།
ལྷ་མོས་གླུ་དབྱངས་ལེན་པ།།
མཛེས་མའི་རང་གཤིས་ཡིན་རུང་།།
འདོད་ལྡན་ལྷ་བུས་ཉོན་དང་།།
སེམས་ལ་ངེས་པར་ཕན་ཡོད།།

སྟོང་གསལ་ནམ་མཁའི་ཁམས་ཀྱི།།
ངོ་མཚར་ཆུ་འཛིན་གསེབ་ན།།
གཡུ་འབྲུག་སྒྲ་དབྱངས་སྒྲོག་པ།།
འབྲུག་གི་རང་གཤིས་ཡིན་རུང་།།
མདངས་ལྡན་རྨ་བྱས་ཉོན་དང་།།
སེམས་ལ་ངེས་པར་ཕན་ཡོད།།

འཛམ་གླིང་གངས་དཀར་ཏི་སེའི།།
ངོ་མཚར་རྫུ་འཕྲུལ་ཕུག་ན།།
རྣལ་འབྱོར་གླུ་དབྱངས་ལེན་པ།།
རྟོགས་ལྡན་རང་གཤིས་ཡིན་རུང་།།
དད་ལྡན་སློབ་མས་ཉོན་དང་།།
སེམས་ལ་ངེས་པར་ཕན་ཡོད།།

I bow to the guru.

In the wondrous grove
Of Ganden, the land of the gods,
Female deities sing songs.
This is the nature of beautiful women.
Desirous sons of deities—listen!
The songs will certainly inspire you.

Among the wondrous clouds
In the expanse of the empty, luminous sky,
A turquoise thunder-dragon calls out melodious sounds.
This is the nature of dragons.
Peacocks with eyes in your feathers—listen!
The sounds will certainly inspire you.

In a wondrous, miraculous cave
On the world's white snow mountain, Tise,
A yogi is singing songs.
This is the nature of realized ones.
Faithful disciples—listen!
The songs will certainly inspire you.

རྒྱལ་པོས་བདག་རྗེན་ཆེན་པོ།།
གནང་རུང་ངོ་མཚར་མི་སྣང་།།
མཚན་ལྡན་བླ་མས་ཟབ་རྒྱའི།།
གདམས་པ་གནང་ན་ངོ་མཚར།།

གནམ་ལ་འཕུར་བའི་བྱ་ཞིག།
ཟིན་རུང་ངོ་མཚར་མི་སྣང་།།
བླ་མས་གདམས་ངག་གནང་བ།།
བློ་ལ་ཟིན་ན་ངོ་མཚར།།

རི་དང་བྲག་གཉིས་སྦྲད་ནས།།
འཕྲོད་རུང་ངོ་མཚར་མི་སྣང་།།
བླ་མས་སེམས་ངོ་སྤྲོད་ནས།།
རང་ངོ་འཕྲོད་ན་ངོ་མཚར།།

སྲ་བའི་ཤིང་ཞིག་བཀུག་ནས།།
ཁུགས་རུང་ངོ་མཚར་མི་སྣང་།།
རང་སེམས་རྒྱོང་པོ་ནང་དུ།།
བཀུག་ནས་ཁུགས་ན་ངོ་མཚར།།

A king granting rewards for service
Is not wondrous.
A qualified lama granting vast and profound instruction
Is wondrous.

Catching a bird flying in the sky
Is not wondrous.
Memorizing oral instruction given by a lama
Is wondrous.

Moving a rock to a mountain
Is not wondrous.
Realizing the nature of mind when a lama points it out
Is wondrous.

Grasping a thick tree with one's arms and bending it
Is not wondrous.
Embracing the tough mind from within so it becomes humble
Is wondrous.

ལྷུགས་ཀྱུས་གླང་ཆེན་སྨྱོན་པ།།
བཏུལ་རུང་ངོ་མཚར་མི་སྣང་།།
ཆོས་ཀྱིས་བདག་འཛིན་ཞུང་རྒྱན།།
བཏུལ་ནས་ཐུལ་ན་ངོ་མཚར།།

ཧ་ཡི་སྙིང་དུ་ཡངས་ནས།།
ཆགས་རུང་ངོ་མཚར་མི་སྣང་།།
སྒོམ་ཆེན་སྙན་གྱི་སྙིང་དུ།།
ཡུན་རིང་ཆགས་ན་ངོ་མཚར།།

འཇིག་རྟེན་པ་ཡི་གླུ་དབྱངས།།
སྙན་ཡང་ངོ་མཚར་མི་སྣང་།།
དམ་པའི་ཆོས་ཀྱི་མགུར་དབྱངས།།
འདི་འདྲ་བླངས་ན་ངོ་མཚར།།

ཞེས་པ་འདི་ཡང་ཉིན་ཞིག་སེམས་ལ་ཤར་བ་ལྟར་བྲིས་པའོ།།

Taming a mad elephant with an iron hook
Is not wondrous.
Subduing the arch-enemy—grasping at a self—with the Dharma
so it grows tame
Is wondrous.

Mounting a horse and staying on it
Is not wondrous.
A yogi remaining on a meditation cushion for a long time
Is wondrous.

A worldly song pleasing the ear
Is not wondrous.
Singing *gur* melodies like this about the holy Dharma
Is wondrous.

I wrote this one day, just as it came to mind.

ན་མོ་གུ་རུ།

གཡུ་འབྲུག་སྔོན་མོ་དེ་ཡང་།།
ས་ལ་བབས་ན་མི་མཛེས།།
ཆུ་འཛིན་གསེབ་ཏུ་བསྡད་ནས།།
སྒྲ་དབྱངས་བསྒྲགས་ན་མཛེས་སོ།།

དར་སེང་དཀར་མོ་དེ་ཡང་།།
ཤོད་དུ་བབས་ན་མི་མཛེས།།
གངས་དཀར་ལྷོངས་སུ་འབྲིངས་ནས།།
ང་རོ་བསྒྲགས་ན་མཛེས་སོ།།

བྱ་བཏང་རྣལ་འབྱོར་དེ་ཡང་།།
གྲོང་དུ་འཁྱམས་ན་མི་མཛེས།།
དབེན་པར་ཉམས་ལེན་བྱས་ནས།།
མགུར་དབྱངས་བླངས་ན་མཛེས་སོ།།

ཞེས་པ་འདི་ཡང་ཚོགས་དྲུག་རང་གྲོལ་གྱིས་བླངས་པའོ།།

I bow to the guru.

If the turquoise blue thunder-dragon
Descends to the ground, he is not beautiful.
When he stays among the clouds
And proclaims melodious sounds, he is beautiful.

If the white snow lion
Descends to the valley, he is not beautiful.
When he poses dauntingly on the summits of snowy mountains
And roars, he is beautiful.

If the renunciant yogi
Roves about in villages, he is not beautiful.
When he practices the Dharma in solitary places
And sings songs of realization, he is beautiful.

Tshogdruk Rangdrol sang this also.

ན་མོ་གུ་རུ།

ནམ་ཟླ་དགུན་དཔྱིད་དེ་བཞུད་ཐལ།།
དབྱར་ཟླ་གསུམ་པོ་ཕོ་སླེབས་བྱུང་།།
ཁུ་བྱུག་སྔོན་མོ་ངའི་སྐྱིད་པ།།
གཤོག་སྒྲོ་ལེགས་པོ་བྱས་བརྒྱངས་ཏེ།།
ལྗོན་ཤིང་རྩེ་མོ་རུ་བབས་ནས།།
བྱ་བྱེའུ་སྣ་ཚོགས་ལ་ལྟ་བཞིན།།
སྐད་སྙན་ཡག་པོ་དེ་འབྱིན་ཡ།།
སྐད་སྙན་ཡག་པོ་ཞིག་འབྱུང་བ།།
ནམ་མཁའི་ལྷོ་སྤྲིན་ནས་སྦྲང་ཆར།།
འཇམ་པོ་བབས་པའི་དྲིན་ཡིན་སྙམ།།
ཁུ་བྱུག་སྔོན་མོ་ང་དགའ་ནས།།
བར་བར་བཞད་གད་རེ་ཤོར་རོ།།

མཚོ་དར་དཀར་བོ་དེ་བཞུད་ཐལ།།
མཚོ་ཆུ་སྔོན་མོ་ནི་སླེབས་བྱུང་།།
དང་བ་སེར་བོ་ངའི་སྐྱིད་པ།།
གཤོག་སྒྲོ་ལེགས་པོ་བྱས་བརྒྱངས་ཏེ།།
མཚོ་ཆུ་སྔོན་མོའི་ཁར་བབས་ནས།།
གསེར་མིག་ཉ་མོ་ལ་ལྟ་བཞིན།།
སྐད་སྙན་ཡག་པོ་དེ་སྒྲོག་ཡ།།

I bow to the guru.

The seasons of winter and spring have passed,
And the three months of summer have arrived.
I, a blue cuckoo, am happy.
Spreading my strong wings,
I glide down to the top of a tree,
And looking at many other birds, big and small,
I send forth rich, sonorous notes. Hey!
I think that the sound of my pleasant voice
Is the kindness of the soft, gentle rain that fell
From the southern clouds in the sky.
I, a blue cuckoo, rejoice,
And from time to time some laughter escapes from within.

The white silk of the lake is gone,
And the blue water of the lake has arrived.
I, a golden duck, am happy.
Spreading my strong wings,
I glide down to the surface of the blue water of the lake,
And looking at the golden-eyed fish
I call out with a fine, resonant voice. Hey!

སྐད་སྙན་ཡག་པོ་ཞིག་བྱུང་བ།།
མཚོ་ཞབས་རྗེ་བཟང་རྩུར་ཆགས་པའི།།
ཞིམ་མདངར་འདམ་གཙང་དྲིན་ཡིན་སྙམ།།
ངང་བ་སེར་པོ་ང་དགའ་ནས།།
བར་བར་གཤོག་སྒྲོ་རེ་སྤྲུགས་སོ།།

བྲིད་ཟླུགས་རྣམ་རྟོག་དེ་ལངས་ཐལ།།
སྟོང་གསལ་རྗེན་པ་པོ་སླེབས་བྱུང་།།
བློ་བཟང་རིན་ཆེན་ངའི་སྙིང་པ།།
ལུས་གནད་ལེགས་པོ་བྱས་བཅོས་ཏེ།།
རྩེ་གཅིག་མཉམ་བཞག་ལ་གནས་ནས།།
གསལ་འདེབས་དཔེ་ཆ་ལ་ལྟ་བཞིན།།
མགུར་དབྱངས་སྙན་མོ་དེ་ལེན་ཡ།།
མགུར་དབྱངས་སྙན་མོ་ཞིག་བྱུང་བ།།
མཚན་ལྡན་བླ་མ་ཡིས་ཟབ་རྒྱུའི།།
གདམས་པ་གནང་བའི་དྲིན་ཡིན་སྙམ།།
བློ་བཟང་རིན་ཆེན་ང་དགའ་ནས།།
བར་བར་ཐལ་མོ་རེ་སྦྲུར་རོ།།

ཞེས་པ་འདི་ཡང་ཉིན་ཞིག་སློབ་བུ་བློ་བཟང་རིན་ཆེན་གྱིས་བསྐུར་བའི་ལན་དུ།

I think that my sonorous voice
Is the kindness of the pure, delicious mud
Which clings to the good stones on the bottom of the lake.
I, a golden duck, rejoice,
And from time to time I shake my feathers.

The heavy fog of conceptual thought has lifted
And fresh, empty clarity has arrived.
I, Lobzang Rinchen, am happy.
Preparing the essential points of physical posture,
I abide single-pointedly in meditative equipoise.
Then, looking at my manual of brief reminders,
I sing a fine-sounding *gur.* Hey!
I think that the arising of a pleasant *gur*
Is the kindness of the qualified lama
Who gave me deep instruction.
I, Lobzang Rinchen rejoice,
And from time to time join my palms.

I sang this one day, in reply to the petition by my disciple, Lobzang Rinchen.

ཨེ་མ་ཧོ།

དབྱངས་སྙན་ཀ་ལ་པིངྐའི་ཕྲུ་གུ་ང༎
ཕ་ཡུལ་སྒོ་ངའི་སྦུབས་ལས་ཐོན་ནས་ཀྱང་༎
ཐོས་བསམ་སྒོམ་གསུམ་འདབ་གཤོག་ལེགས་བརྒྱངས་ནས༎
ཡིད་འོང་དབེན་པའི་དཔག་བསམ་ལྗོན་ཤིང་རྩེར༎
འཕུར་ནས་ལེགས་བཤད་ཆོས་ཀྱི་སྒྲ་དབྱངས་དེ༎
ལྷང་ལྷང་ཕྱོགས་བཅུར་ཡོངས་སུ་སྒྲོག་པ་ཡིན༎

ཡིད་འཕྲོག་ཤིན་ཏུ་སྙན་པའི་དབྱངས་སྙན་འདིས༎
གཞན་ཡིད་ཕྲོགས་ནས་ལྗོན་ཤིང་རྩེར་འཛེག་ཤོག༎

ཅེས་དེ་རྣམས་ཀྱི་ཕྱོགས་སུ་བལྟས་ནས་བརྩེ་བའི་སེམས་ཀྱིས་དེ་རྣམས་འཁོར་བའི་བྱ་བ་བུ་དང་ཆུང་མར་སྐྲ་ཙམ་ཡང་མི་ཆགས་པར་ལས་ཅན་མང་པོ་དབེན་པར་ང་ཕྱིར་འབྲངས་ནས་ཉམས་ལེན་བྱེད་པར་གྱུར་ཅིག་ཅེས་སྨོན་ལམ་ལེགས་པར་བཏབ་བོ༎

Oh!

I, a *kalavinka* chick with sweet melodies,

Emerged from the confines of my homeland, an eggshell,

And spreading my strong wings of learning, contemplating
and meditating,

I flew to the top of the wish-fulfilling tree in a delightful, solitary place,

And am calling out in the ten directions with a full, clear voice

A song of lucid exposition of the Dharma.

May this very enchanting, melodious voice of mine

Captivate the minds of others, and may they ascend to the top of the tree.

Looking in their direction with loving thoughts, I prayed deeply, "May many fortunate ones follow me to a solitary place and become practitioners of the Dharma, without being attached in the slightest to activities in samsara, a child or a mate."

Appendices

Abbreviations

BT Cook, Elizabeth and the Yeshe De Project, under the direction of Tarthang Tulku. *The Buddha and His Teachings*. In *Crystal Mirror Series*. Vol. 10. Berkeley, Calif.: Dharma Publishing, 1995.

CL Chris Leahy of the Massachusetts Audubon Society, interviews by author, e-mails, winter, 2006–2007.

EB Buswell, Robert E., Jr., ed. *Encyclopedia of Buddhism*. New York: Macmillan Reference USA, 2004.

Geshe TC Geshe Tsultrim Chopel of the Kurukulla Center in Malden, MA, interviews by author, notes, spring, 2008.

IW1 Waldo, Ives. Entries in *The Rangjung Yeshe Gilded Palace of Dharmic Activity*. http://rywiki.tsadra.org.

IW2 Waldo, Ives. The dictionary of Ives Waldo. Accessed via the Tibetan Translation Tool, http://www.thdl.org/tools/download.html?free_dict.

JV Valby, Jim. The dictionary of Jim Valby, accessed via the Tibetan Translation Tool, http://www.thdl.org/tools/download.html?free_dict.

LC Lobzang Chödrag, scholar in Rebgong, Amdo, interviews by author, notes, summer, 2006.

PH Padma Gyurmed Namgyal, Zhechen Gyaltsab. *Path of Heroes: Birth of Enlightenment: With the Practice Instructions and Reflections of Tarthang Tulku*. Translated by Deborah Black. Vol. 2. Berkeley, Calif.: Dharma Publishing, 1995.

RY1 Rangjung Yeshe. Entries in *The Rangjung Yeshe Gilded Palace of Dharmic Activity*. http://rywiki.tsadra.org.

RY2 Rangjung Yeshe. *The Rangjung Yeshe Tibetan-English Dictionary of Buddhist Culture*. Accessed via the Tibetan Translation Tool, http://www.thdl.org/tools/download.html?free_dict.

SH	Zhabs dkar Tshogs drug rang grol, 1781–1851. *The Life of Shabkar: The Autobiography of a Tibetan Yogin*. Translated by Matthieu Ricard, et al. Albany: State University of New York Press, 1994.
Skal ldan, *Mgur 'bum*	Skal ldan rgya mtsho. *Shar skal ldan rgya mtsho'i mgur 'bum.* Xining: Mtsho sngon mi rigs dpe skrun khang, 1994.
TBRC	The Tibetan Buddhist Resource Center. E. Gene Smith, Executive Director. http://www.tbrc.org
TTC	*Bod rgya tshig mdzod chen mo*. Beijing: Mi rigs dpe skrun khang, 1993.
VS	Sujata, Victoria. *Tibetan Songs of Realization: Echoes from a Seventeenth-Century Scholar and Siddha in Amdo*. Leiden: Brill, 2005.
WE	[Dharma Publishing staff, under the guidance of Tarthang Tulku.] *Ways of Enlightenment: Buddhist Studies at Nyingma Institute*. Berkeley, Calif.: Dharma Publishing, 1993.
ZH	Zhabs dkar Tshogs drug rang grol. *Rje zhabs dkar tshogs drug rang grol gyi gsung 'bum.* Vol. 1. Xining: Mtsho sngon mi rigs dpe skrun khang, 2002. (This is the biography of Shabkar. Please see my bibliography for its full title.)
Zhabs dkar, *Gsung 'bum*	Zhabs dkar Tshogs drug rang grol. [*Bya btang tshogs drug rang grol gyis rang dang skal ldan gdul bya la mgrin pa gdams pa'i bang mdzod nas glu dbyangs dga' ston 'gyed pa rnams.*] In *Rje zhabs dkar tshogs drug rang grol gyi gsung 'bum*. Vols. 3–4. Xining: Mtsho sngon mi rigs dpe skrun khang, 2002. (This is a collection of *gur* by Shabkar.)

Languages

T	Tibetan
S	Sanskrit
C	Chinese

While I have paraphrased definitions from my sources, or chosen certain terms from their lists, any errors are my own.

Notes

Chapter 1. Lamas

5 None of the colophons of the gur I have translated here from Shabkar's collection of songs use a pronoun to refer to the author, so the question arises whether **Shabkar** wrote his own **colophons** or whether someone else wrote them for him. I have tentatively translated them in the first person, because it is clear that he wrote other works down himself. M. Ricard tells us that manuscripts of various of Shabkar's works still exist today in his own handwriting (*SH*, 577). Shabkar himself tells us in the introduction to his autobiography that he wrote down notes on his life, and later wrote down the autobiography (*SH*, 5, 7). M. Ricard believes that Shabkar's songs were written down on the occasion in which they were sung (*SH*, xix), and various colophons state that when those gur came to mind, they were immediately put down in writing (i.e. Zhabs dkar, *Gsung 'bum* 4: 503, 513, 546). Furthermore, the colophons rarely include honorific language, and when they do, it is in reference to someone the author respects, not the author.

This song is also translated by M. Ricard in "The Writings of Shabkar: A Descriptive Catalogue," in *Zhabs dkar tshogs drug rang grol gyi bka' 'bum: The Collected Works of Zhabs dkar tshogs drug rang grol (1781–1851)* (New Delhi: Shechen Publications, 2003), 9.

For a discussion of **similes** as indigenous Tibetan poetic figures, see VS, 189–205.

9 **Ngawang Lobzang Tendzin Rinpoche** (1745–1812) was one of Shabkar's teachers. Born in Amdo, he went to the famed Nyingmapa monastery Mindroling (T: Smin grol gling) in Central Tibet, and received the empowerments of that tradition. Later, he give those empowerments to Shabkar in Amdo (*SH*, 35, n. 11).

The **royal white vulture** is the Himalayan Griffon, which becomes very pale as an adult (CL).

11 This gur is written in the style of **parallelism**, an indigenous Tibetan poetic figure that is used frequently in gur. For an explanation of parallelism, more examples, and commentary about parallelism as an indigenous Tibetan poetic figure, see VS, 217–22.

For a discussion of **quatrains** and **stanza external repetition**, see VS, 140–47.

13 **Wutaishan** (= C; T: Ri bo rtse lnga) is the famed pilgrimage site with five peaks in northern China (see map 1) thought to be the home of Mañjuśrī, the bodhisattva of wisdom, and a place of pilgrimage devoted to his homage.

15 For a similar song of farewell employing parallelism, see *SH*, 101; *ZH*: 198–99.

17 Metaphors that involve the **sun** usually have to do with the Buddha, his teachings, the wisdom of one's lama, or his compassion. The sun can also refer to the nature of mind, or to happiness. For a discussion of the metaphor **sun rising**, see VS, 206, 211–13.

Lotuses are metaphors for feet. LC believes that this is because the lotus is considered an ornament, such as when women wear lotuses in their hair. When someone who bows to a lama puts the lama's feet on his head, it is like putting a lotus ornament in his hair (LC).

Chögyäl Ngakyi Wangpo (1736–1807; T: Chos rgyal Ngag dbang wang po) is Shabkar's main teacher. For a concise biography of him, see *SH*, xxii–xxiii.

For a similar song in which Shabkar sings of being inspired to recall his lama's body, speech, mind, and other qualities by things he sees in nature, see *SH*, 54–55; *ZH*, 103–4.

Chapter 2. Impermanence

23 I would like to thank CL for suggesting ways to describe the sounds of **waterbirds**, as well as those of cuckoos, ducks, geese, sparrows, and Indian cuckoos, below. Shabkar usually describes the voices of the various birds as skad snyan (T), translated in dictionaries as a melodious, sweet-sounding, eloquent, pleasant voice (RY1, IW1, RY2, IW2). But those definitions are too narrow, and I take skad snyan to mean a good voice for whatever type of bird to which it applies. The sounds of the shorebirds and geese at **Lake Kokonor** range from melancholic piping or yodeling to harsh quacking and squawking (CL). The waterbirds there would certainly not be calling out sweetly or melodiously, or even necessarily pleasingly.

Lake Kokonor is the huge lake in central Amdo also known in various languages as the Blue Lake, Qinghai Hu, **Tsho Ngönpo** and **Trishor Gyälmo.** For the location of Lake Kokonor, see maps 1 and 2.

27 **Chökyi Gyälpo**. *See* Chögyäl Ngakyi Wangpo, above.

Jamyang Gyatso Rinpoche (d. 1800; T: 'Jam dbyangs rgya mtsho) was also one of Shabkar's main teachers.

The arising of kyowa (T: skyo ba) or kyo she (skyo shas), **disenchantment or disillusion with the world**, is considered very positive, since it inspires one to continue to let go of things that are impermanent anyway.

29 All sentient beings are believed to have been one's **mothers in former lives**. Hence one should have compassion for all beings and a desire for their enlightenment, just as one would for one's biological mother.

Chapter 3. Passing Away of Mother and Father

33 This song is also found in the autobiography. For M. Ricard's rendering, see *SH*, 201–2; *ZH*, 413–14. There are some differences in the original Tibetan as well as in the translations. For a similar song, see *SH*, 494; *ZH*, 1011–12.

Seen from another side, in Shabkar's autobiography we learn that he intentionally lied to his mother when he was leaving home, when he promised to return to her after one year (*SH*, 40–43). He did not return to see her for more than seven years, though she was ill and needed his help. He criticized himself for feeling attached to her:

> Just to meet your mother in person is pointless,
> And might make problems—so forget it!

and gave himself advice on how to meet her in the absolute state (*SH*, 73–74). For a letter from his mother begging him to come home to visit once more before she dies, see *SH*, 140–41; *ZH*, 290–91; and his response to her in *SH*, 141–42; *ZH*, 291–93.

37 For other songs in which Shabkar expresses grief over not meeting his mother again, see Zhabs dkar, *Gsung 'bum* 4: 420–22; *SH*, 494; *ZH*, 1011–12. For a dream he had of his mother living in the Western Buddha-field, see *SH*, 499; *ZH*, 1023–24.

43 **Ütsang**, or **Ü** and **Tsang** (T: Dbus gtsang) are the two main provinces of Central Tibet. *See* map 1.

The form of this song is quite similar to some by Kälden Gyatso (1607–1677; T: Skal ldan rgya mtsho), a scholar and siddha whose main hermitage was on the opposite side of Rongbo Valley from that of Shabkar. *See*, for example, Skal ldan, *Mgur 'bum*, 142–43, and 147–49. All three have a repetition of the third line of each of their stanzas, and Shabkar uses the exact same line that Kälden Gyatso uses in the former. In the fourth lines of the three songs, each author concludes that he will not remain where he is, and must leave for some hermitage.

Shabkar is influenced both stylistically and spiritually by the songs of Kälden Gyatso, receives an oral transmission of his *Collection of Songs*, and sings his songs. Shabkar also shows affinity with the former scholar and yogi by going to places where Kälden Gyatso had meditated, and expresses the hope to also stay someday in mountain retreats. *See SH*, 15, 21–22 n. 2, 29, 71, 137, 146, 493, 502, 528, 529.

Before.... Now..... For a discussion of **antithesis** as an indigenous Tibetan poetic figure, see VS, 222–23.

This song is also found in the autobiography. For M. Ricard's translation, see *SH*, 205–6; *ZH*, 422–23.

51 Money or many other things can be given as **ransom** in the Tibetan tradition, to appease evil spirits in order to restore health.

Chapter 4. Nature

59 In my translations I am usually able to translate rgod (T) literally as **vulture**. However, in this case and one other, I have followed M. Ricard's example in translating rgod as **eagle** rather than vulture, because of the negative connotation of the vulture in the West (*SH*).

But the vulture is actually considered an auspicious bird in Tibet, where it participates in one's final act of compassion in a lifetime: donating one's body for the benefit of other beings via a sky burial, in which the vulture is fed the softer parts. Interestingly, it seems that from a Tibetan spiritual view, the eagle is the bird from this pair to be pitied, because it is trapped in a lifetime of violently killing live animals, whereas the vulture has a good reputation because it rarely kills live animals for food, and partakes in the rituals mentioned above. (*See* the line, "Oh yeah! The sinful hawk has arrived," in the chapter on hermitage, pp. 173–75.) CL has told me that there are some magnificent vultures in Tibet, especially the Lammergeier, which eats bone marrow, and the Himalayan Griffon.

CL has also pointed out that the term "vulture," as used in the Americas, does not have precisely the same meaning as the vulture of Europe, Asia, and Africa, which is essentially a "carrion-eating eagle." So ornithology does not distinguish strongly between vultures and eagles in Tibet, where both exist throughout, and the local people may not either (CL).

The other song in which I have chosen to substitute "eagle" for "vulture" is marked in the notes, and also involves a case in which the sense of the vulture as a simile or metaphor is too easily misinterpreted by our culture. If any vulture enthusiasts disagree with my substitutions, please know that you can have the last laugh: "certain species of eagles in Tibet are also likely to join in on the carrion feast along with their vulturine relatives" (CL).

Here Shabkar uses the same metaphor of a bird flying into the dharmadhātu (T: chos kyi dbyings) as in a gur by Kälden Gyatso. *See* dharmadhātu in the glossary. *See also* VS, 364–69; Skal ldan, *Mgur 'bum*, 223–24, for Kälden Gyatso's gur.

dragon (T: 'brug) is a metaphor for thunder. I have followed M. Ricard's example of translating it as thunder-dragon in *SH*.

The **summer drum** is also a metaphor for thunder.

I have seen several references in gur to **peacocks** and **thunder**. A Tibetan friend says he saw peacocks fanning open their tails and strutting around with delight during a thunderstorm, making him think that peacocks love thunder, though CL seems quite doubtful about this.

61 **Rain** is frequently used as a metaphor or simile in gur from Amdo, where water is scarce. Rain is almost always equated with desirable things that one's lama grants in abundance, such as spiritual powers, teachings, and blessings. For the metaphor of **rain**, see VS, 206, 207–8, 213. For the simile **fall like rain**, see VS, 189, 193–95.

For another song about seeing spiritual lessons in nature, see *SH*, 406–7; *ZH*, 826–27.

67 **Tshonying** is an island in Lake Kokonor. *See* map 2.

73 For a discussion of **interjections** as indigenous Tibetan poetic figures, see VS, 228–46. **Hey!** (T: ya) is discussed on pp. 236–37.

75 **That her paternal aunt of wrongdoing**
Did not torment her is good. Hey!
Paternal aunts are frequently considered evil in Tibetan lay literature.

For a quite similar gur, see VS, 288–95; Skal ldan, *Mgur 'bum*, 71–72. For a discussion of **metaphors** as indigenous Tibetan poetic figures, see VS, 206–17. For a comparison with verse in the biography of Marpa compiled by Tsang Nyön Heruka (T: Gtsang smyon He ru ka), see p. 216.

Chapter 5. Death

79 **I will now give advice to all who hear this song.**
I felt a need to add this line to clarify that Shabkar has moved from addressing his lama to addressing his students.

83 For other songs about how one must recall death and prepare for it, see *SH*, 212–13; *ZH*, 438–40; and *SH*, 409–10; *ZH*, 833–35.

89 When Shabkar refers to **Tashikhyil**, it's **Yama Tashikhyil** (T: G.ya ma Bkra shis 'khyil). For a description of Shabkar's lovely hermitage to the east of Rongbo Valley, see *SH*, 496–97; *ZH*, 1018–20. It was founded by Gendun Tenpai Nyima (T: Rgyal Mkhan chen Dge 'dun Bstan pa'i nyi ma), who may have been born in 1758 (*SH*, 12 n. 22; TBRC). Two other Tashikhyil's are nearby. **(Rongbo) Tashikhyil** (T: Rong bo Bkra shis 'khyil) was Kälden Gyatso's main hermitage high above Rongbo Valley, to the west. Kälden Gyatso founded a school of tantric studies there in 1648 (Byang chub mi la Ngag dbang bsod nams, *Grub chen skal ldan rgya mtsho'i rnam thar*, 31). The very famous **Ladrang Tashikhyil** was founded by Jamyang Shepai Dorje ('Jam dbyangs bzhad pa'i rdo rje) in 1709, between the foundings of Rongbo Tashikhyil and Yama Tashikhyil. It is located beyond Yama Tashikhyil, farther to the east. Because of the geographical proximity of the three sites, it seems that the names for Yama Tashikhyil and Ladrang Tashikhyil are related to the name of Kälden Gyatso's hermitage. For the location of Yama Tashikhyil, see maps 1 and 2. For Rongbo Tashikhyil and Ladrang Tashikhyil, see map 2.

Chapter 6. Renunciation

111 **Salung** (T: Zwa lung) is possibly a typographical error for Shalung (T: Zhwa lung), a place near Lhasa where Shabkar lived in retreat for a year. For his stay at Zhwa lung, see *SH*, 232.

115 Padmasaṃbhava is said to have been born in Oḍḍiyāna, an area probably in the northwest of India, of which **Ogyen** is a corruption (*EB*, RY2). *See also* Padmasaṃbhava in the glossary.

117 For another song about the benefits of renunciation, see *SH*, 413–14; *ZH*, 839–40.

Chapter 7. Old Age

121 My dictionaries and LC translate ze ba (T) as mane, but dragons do not have manes, so I have translated ze ba here tentatively as **claws**, according to context. LC also feels that translating ze ba this way is the best choice.

123 One of the highest ideals and motivating forces in Mahāyāna Buddhism is to **be of unlimited service to the Buddhist teachings and all sentient beings**.

131 There are lots of nesting birds at the Kokonor, but also lots of birds that migrate through in the spring and fall. Some species, such as shorebirds, leave precisely at the same time each year. Others, such as ducks, stay as long as there is still a part of the lake that is free from ice (CL).

133 **This body, a necessary support for practicing the Dharma,**
has aged, and is passing by.
One evening, on the slope of the mountain Magyäl,
I found a horse of disillusionment with the world, and am riding it.
At this very moment as I am urging him on with this crop of a well-sounding *gur*,
He is carrying me on the path of deep, vast spirituality, and is passing by.

Shabkar tells us that while he is dying, he is urging his mind on towards the Dharma by singing a gur. Now even disillusionment with the world passes by.

Magyäl (T: Rma rgyal) is another name for **Amnye Machen** (T: A myes rma chen), a mountain range in Amdo to the south of Lake Kokonor. *See* maps 1 and 2.

Chapter 8. Self-Criticism

137 I have interpreted the unexpressed object of "lama, possessed of the three," to be kindnesses. There are two sets of **three kindnesses**, and the reference refers ambiguously to either (LC). *See* three kindnesses in the glossary.

143 For other songs with scathing self-criticism, see *SH*, 383–85; *ZH*, 787–90; and *SH*, 415–16; *ZH*, 843–44 (by a disciple of his).

Chapter 9. Nonsectarianism

149 **Machen** refers to **Amnye Machen** (T: A myes rma chen). *See* above.

151 I have substituted "**eagle**" for "vulture" in this song.

153 For another song about great masters departing this earth, see *SH*, 120; *ZH*, 244–45.

159 For other songs about **nonsectarianism**, see *SH*, 138; *ZH*, 281–82; *SH*, 432; *ZH*, 878; Skal ldan, *Mgur 'bum*, 266–68; 172–73.

Chapter 10. Hermitage

167 The metaphor **blazing or fiery pit** is used in gur to refer to the dangers of samsara, which need to be watched like a fiery pit.

175 **Kälden Repa** (T: Skal ldan ras pa) is Kälden Gyatso, a name Kälden Gyatso also uses for himself in some of his colophons. *See* repa in the glossary.

179 The similarities of the preceding song by Shabkar to a song by Kälden Gyatso are obvious. I present Kälden Gyatso's here, so that the reader can see the two side by side. For an earlier translation of Kälden Gyatso's song, see VS, 296–310, which is discussed on pp. 241–45. Other aspects of Shabkar's song, such as the same progression of interjections, and the exact last line, are found elsewhere in Kälden Gyatso's songs.

183 I have come across various references to a deity named **Mahādeva** who lives at Lake Kokonor, but I have not found out who it is. Although Mahādeva is a name for Śiva, I have been told that the deity at the Kokonor is not Śiva (LC).

The story about a **lion growing a mane** is an old folk tale. In this tale, a lion that does not climb to the top of a glacier can not grow a long mane (LC).

189 **And Kälden, who dispelled the darkness in Rebgong,**
Rebgong is an area in eastern Amdo where many of the songs in this book may have been written. Its boundaries have changed over time. *See* map 2.

"Kälden" is Kälden Gyatso.

191 The continual use of "**because...., I am happy**" (T: "pas bde") at the end of a line is a form found frequently in gur that the songwriter uses to list reasons why he is happy. *See also* two gur in the chapter on happiness which employ this form, found on pp. 233–35 and pp. 247–49. *See also* Skal ldan, *Mgur 'bum*, 152–53; VS, 346–51; and VS, 225 n. 116, which gives references for this form in songs of Milarepa.

For a discussion of a **continual repetition of a finite verb** as an indigenous Tibetan poetic figure, see VS, 224–26.

Chapter 11. Meditation Experiences

207 **Living joyfully....** (T: dga' yal le// ....)
This stanza is made up of phrases Shabkar exclaims to describe his experiences as he lets his mind go. He is playing with sounds here—perhaps imitating the sounds of the horse's hooves galloping—dga' yal le// skyid chil le// ban ma bun// phya ma 'phyo// 'al ma 'ol// shag ma shig/ khral ma khrol// sangs ma sangs// ya la la// yengs yengs yengs// ye re re// phyam phyam phyam// me re re// (T). I have translated most of these lines tentatively, with information from RY1 and Geshe TC. I have no clue about two of these phrases (shag ma shig and ye re re), so I have omitted them from my translation for the time being. It was suggested that phyam phyam phyam (T) may be onomatopoeic for the sound of cymbals clashing, or bells ringing, so I have left the line as **sham, sham, sham** (Amdo-dialect pronunciation for the transliteration phyam phyam phyam).

209 **A yo she! E ha ha!** (T: aa yo she// ae ha ha//). By context, these appear to be interjections.

Here Shabkar is referring to relative **bodhicitta**. *See* altruistic aspiration to enlightenment in the glossary.

accumulations. *See* two accumulations in the glossary.

E ma ho (= T) is an interjection of great wonder, surprise, or astonishment. For more, see VS, 231.

This gur is written in a very unusual **meter** with only **three syllables per line**, subdivided into two plus one.

213 The metaphors—**bees** for **mind**, **lotus grove** for **heart cakra**, and **honey** for **profound experience and intuition**—are strengthened by the fact that in many practices one visualizes a lotus in one's heart cakra (LC).

217 **E ma, as for the mind of the renunciant... E ma** (= T; How wonderful/ marvelous!) is an interjection expressing amazement.

They straighten their bodies refers to assuming the **essential points of physical posture**. *See* **seven postures of Vairocana** in the glossary.

219 **The moonlight of the yogis' renown**
Clears away the darkness of delusion of deities and humans.
The lotuses of their disciples' hands close by themselves.

The metaphors continue: lotus is a metaphor for hands. Lotuses close at night, the time the moonlight mentioned above shines. Lotuses open in the daytime with the sunlight (LC).

221 **Tsari** (T: TsA ri), a famous pilgrimage site in Tibet with a mountain around which pilgrims circumambulate, was formerly home to such renowned ascetics as Milarepa and Pema Karpo (1527–1592). Its main peak is Pure Crystal Mountain (Dag pa shel ri). For its location close to the border with Assam, see map 1.

Chapter 12. Happiness

229 **manual of brief reminders,** more literally concise instruction manual with its reminders (T: gsal 'debs be'u bum). The small book of concise oral instructions on what to accept and what to reject (T: be'u bum) also includes reminding instructions (gsal 'debs) (LC).

235 For other songs about happiness by Shabkar, see *SH*, 102–3; *ZH*, 201–4; *SH*, 150–51; *ZH*, 309–10; and *SH*, 370–71; *ZH*, 758–59.

255 Though there are several places called **Arig** (= T) in northeastern Tibet, I have chosen the one near the northeastern shore of Lake Kokonor (see map 2) because it is clear from *SH* that Shabkar frequently went for alms in that area.

Chapter 13. Singing

259 For another gur about songs benefiting others, see *SH*, 251–52; *ZH*, 514–15.

263 **Tise** (= T, Gangs Rin po che; **Mt. Kailash**) in Western Tibet, is the renowned mountain sacred to followers of Buddhism, Hinduism, and Bön alike. According to tradition, Milarepa lived there, so when

a yogi sings songs at Mt. Tise, one recalls Milarepa's life story. For its location far to the west of the Central Tibetan provinces of Ü and Tsang, see map 1.

For another lovely song about singing, composed with parallelism, see *SH*, 251; *ZH*, 513.

273 The **blue cuckoo** seems likely to be the Common (or Eurasian) Cuckoo, with blue-gray feathers, which is frequently found in mountainous areas. CL comments on their songs, which are endlessly repetitive: "It is a haunting sound with an insistent quality as if the bird is anxious to communicate something very important. It tends to take on the mood of the moment. If it is raining, it can sound like a lamentation, but on a bright morning it can sound like a bracing wake up. But it's definitely not a 'pretty bird song'" (CL).

Although there are swans (T: ngang ba) in Tibet, here ngang ba is best translated as **duck**. Since its color is identified as golden (literally, yellow), it is possibly the Ruddy Shelduck, often found in the highlands of Asia. The color of its feathers is similar to that of some Buddhist monks' robes in Southeast Asia, so it has sacred overtones in Buddhist countries and is sometimes called "Buddha Duck" (CL).

Considering a **duck's voice fine and resonant** might be "over flattering," CL jokes. A duck expert describes the sounds of Ruddy Shelduck as follows: "The male has a rather high-pitched nasal whooping call which sounds like a prolonged 'ah-ouk' and also repeated ascending notes, 'ho-ho-ho'. The female is even louder, with a harsher tone, 'Ka-ha-ha'." For this, see Jean Delacour, *The Waterfowl of the World*, vol. 1 (London: Country Life, 1954), 251, cited by CL.

275 Shabkar is singing this gur in the first person, but Lobzang Rinchen is his disciple.

279 **kalavinka** (Tibetanized Sanskrit: ka la pinka, ka la binka) is a Himalayan bird which is renowned for its beautiful voice. Buddhist sutras make numerous references to kalavinkas, which are said to reside in a pure Buddha-field as well as on earth, and whose songs are sometimes metaphors for the Buddha's voice. There are other legends about kalavinkas as well, such as that they can be heard singing from inside their shells, and even—in some Buddhist countries—that they are half human and half bird.

If Shabkar's reference is based on a real bird, it is not clear from Tibetan dictionaries which species it is. Kalapiṅka is defined with a very diverse set of bird types, such as kalapinga bird; sparrow; Indian cuckoo; a warbling bird; a singing bird with a sweet voice; [a] bird living on an ocean island with a beautiful voice (RY1, IW2, JV). However, we do know that the young bird in Shabkar's song has a pleasing, full, clear, melodious voice. Therefore I have avoided translating kalapiṅka as either Indian Cuckoo (a different species from the Common or Eurasian Cuckoo, though very similar), whose voice is not melodious; or sparrow, which sounds either "harsh and chirpy, or buzzy" (CL).

The bird in this song may well be a **lark**, which certainly fits its description (CL), and is among the definitions provided in the Tibetanized Sanskrit-Tibetan dictionary *Sam bod rgya gsum shan sbyar gyi tshig mdzod* (Beijing: Mi rigs dpe skrun khang, 1993). However, since Shabkar does not use the common Tibetan word for lark (lco ga), it seems he wants to invoke a much larger context of associations by using its (Tibetanized) Sanskrit name, in order to strengthen the message of his song. I thank CL, K.E. Duffin, and Ronnie Broadfoot of the Museum of Comparative Zoology at Harvard University for helping me amass this information.

Glossary of Buddhist Terms

Abhirati (T: Mngon dga'; realm of true joy) is the Buddha-field of Akṣobhya (T: Sangs rgyas mi 'khrugs pa). *See* Buddha-field, below.

Akaniṣṭha (T: 'Og min) is the Buddha-field of Vajradhāra (T: Rdo rje 'chang), and the highest Pure Land in existence.

altruistic aspiration to enlightenment (S: **bodhicitta**; T: byang chub kyi sems, byang sems; thought of awakening). Absolute bodhicitta is an awakened understanding that realizes the emptiness of phenomena. Relative bodhicitta is a mind set on practicing the six pāramitās to achieve enlightenment in order to liberate other beings from samsara. Bodhicitta is the unity of wisdom and compassionate skillful means. For more, see *PH*, 260–66; *BT*, 29–35.

Atiśa (b. 972/982–1054; T: Jo bo rje), an adherent of the Prāsaṅgika philosophy, studied at all four of the great Buddhist monasteries in northern India and became the abbot of Vikramaśila. Later, he was one of the most important masters to bring Buddhism to Tibet following the Period of Darkness, at the beginning of the Later Transmission of Dharma. *See EB*, 35–36.

bardo (= T; intermediate state) usually refers to the place where the mind goes after death, for a duration ranging from a split second up to forty-nine days. While the term "bardo" most commonly refers to this state between death and one's next rebirth, it can refer to five other types of intermediate states as well. *See EB*, 377–79.

blessings (T: byin rlabs). It is believed that there are a variety of blessings, or energies, that are always available to be received if one opens with devotion to the Buddhas, bodhisattvas, one's lineage, one's root lama, and so on. The strength of the blessings is a function of the recipient's faith, and of the compassionate commitment on the part of the realized ones to assist all beings in reaching enlightenment.

bodhicitta. *See* altruistic aspiration to enlightenment.

bodhisattva (T: byang chub sems dpa'; one on the path of pursuing awakening) is a practitioner on the Mahāyāna path of compassion and the six pāramitās, who has vowed to attain enlightenment for the benefit of all sentient beings. For a guide to the fundamental training of the bodhisattva see *PH*.

Buddha-field (T: zhing, dag pa'i zhing) is a realm that has been purified or is in the process of being purified by the Buddha or bodhisattva who presides over it and inhabits it. For more, see *EB*, 186–87, 698, 703.

Chenrezig (S: Avalokiteśvara; T: Spyan ras gzigs) is one of the major bodhisattvas, that of compassion, and an emanation of Buddha Amitābha. He is the patron of Tibet.

Completion Stage (T: rdzogs rim, S: saṃpannakrama). Shabkar himself describes the ultimate Completion Stage in his autobiography as follows: "remaining in evenness in the continuum of the nature of mind—void, luminous, free of fixation; all-pervading, open, vast, simple, like the sky" (*SH*, 373).

ḍākinī (T: mkha' 'gro ma; ones who go in the sky), as used in this text, is a sky-going female wrathful or semi-wrathful deity who protects Buddhist teachings in general, and one's spiritual practices in particular. In other contexts, human beings who have attained high realizations as yoginīs, or female tantric practitioners, can also be referred to as ḍākinīs.

definitive meaning (T: nges don). Buddha's teachings that are taught in this mode state their direct meaning. This is in contrast to teachings of provisional meaning, which are adapted to the understanding of specific recipients who have limited levels of comprehension.

Dharma (T: chos) is a term with many definitions, and generally refers to the teachings of the Buddha. Within the context of Shabkar's songs, Dharma can often be translated as "religion" or "religious."

dharmadhātu (T: chos kyi dbyings, real nature of phenomena) is "the absolute expanse: emptiness pervaded with awareness" (*SH*, 91 n. 10).

dharmakāya, or **truth body** (T: chos sku) is described as luminous clarity, unfathomable, immeasurable, inconceivable, incomparable, and immaculate in Arya Maitreya, *Buddha Nature: the Mahayana Uttaratantra Shastra*, 43–52, 182–217 (Ithaca, NY: Snow Lion Publications, 2000); dharmakāya is the ultimate nature of Buddha, "the absolute expanse: emptiness pervaded with awareness" (*SH*, 91 n. 10). For more, see *BT*, 47–54.

dharmapāla (T: chos skyong), in the present text, refers to a spirit or other bodiless being who engages in protection of the Buddhist teachings and their followers. Dharmapālas can also be powerful, ordinary beings.

Dzogchen (S: Mahāsandhi; T: Rdzogs pa chen po or Rdzogs chen; the Great Perfection or Great Completion) is a transmission considered "the pinnacle of the Nyingma tradition and the ultimate view of the nine vehicles. It is based on primordial purity (T: ka dag) and spontaneous presence (lhun grub)" (*SH*, 92 n. 20).

eight worldly concerns or preoccupations (T: chos brgyad) are sometimes translated as attachment to pleasure and aversion to pain, attachment to gain and aversion to loss, attachment to praise and aversion to blame, and attachment to fame and aversion to a bad reputation (T: bde dang mi bde, rnyed dang mi rnyed, bstod dang smad, and snyan dang mi snyan). Though on the conventional level, one of each pair seems good, and the other seems bad, they are all to be transcended. Involvement with the eight worldly concerns keeps beings imprisoned in the realms of samsara.

enjoyment body. *See* three bodies of the Buddha, sambhogakāya.

five poisons (S: kleśa; T: dug lnga, nyon mongs) are emotional obscurations that obscure clarity of perception and ultimately produce suffering. They are desire (T: 'dod chags), anger (zhe sdang), lack of discernment (gti mug), pride (nga rgyal), and envy (phra dog).

flower ball (T: bcud len). Eating only prepared balls of flowers is one of an assortment of the ascetic practices called rasāyana.

four principles of virtuous training (T: dge sbyong gi chos bzhi) are doctrines of a spiritual ascetic for training in virtue. They are: "not to hate others despite being the object of their hatred, not to retaliate in anger even when angry, not to injure others even when injured, and not to beat others even when one is beaten by them" (IW2).

free of fixation (T: 'dzin med; non-fixation, non-grasping, non-clinging, free of fixation, not fixating) is the state of not fixating on distinctions such as subject and object.

Ganden (S: Tuṣita; T: Dga' ldan) is the Buddha-field of the Buddha Maitreya (T: Byams pa).

garuḍa (T: khyung) is a large bird found in Indian mythology that is said to prey on snakes and even to be able to carry elephants away (CL). It hatches fully grown.

Generation Stage, or **Development Stage** (T: bskyed rim, S: utpattikrama) is a type of Tantrayāna meditation involving mantra repetition and visualization of a deity in order to actualize in oneself the nature of the deity.

Glorious Copper-Colored Mountain (T: Zangs mdog dpal gyi ri) is the Buddha-field of Padmasaṃbhava. *See* Padmasaṃbhava, below.

Great Compassionate One (S: Mahākāruṇika; T: Thugs rje chen po) is a name for Chenrezig (T: Spyan ras gzigs). *See* Chenrezig, above.

gur (T: mgur) is a song of spiritual realization or experience.

higher realms are those one can take birth in as a human, demigod, or god.

human body with freedoms and advantages refers to the conditions within a **free and well-favored human birth** (T: dal 'byor mi lus). A human birth with the so-called eight freedoms and the ten advantages or favorable conditions is highly valued because one has all necessary conditions for Dharma practice. "The **freedoms from eight obstacles** to practicing the Dharma ... are 1) to be born in a hell realm, 2) among the pretas, or tormented spirits, 3) as an animal, 4) among savages, 5) as a long-living god, 6) holding totally erroneous views, 7) in a dark kalpa, during which no Buddha has appeared in the world, 8) with impaired sense faculties" (*SH*, 602). "... Among the **ten favorable conditions**, there are five conditions that depend on ourselves (T: rang 'byor lnga): 1) to be born as a human being, 2) in a place where the Dharma flourishes, 3) with complete sense faculties, 4) without the karma of living in a way totally opposite to the Dharma, 5) and having faith in what deserves it. There are five conditions that depend upon others (gzhan 'byor lnga): 1) a Buddha should have appeared in the world, 2) and have taught the

Dharma, 3) the Dharma should have remained until our days, 4) we should have entered the Dharma, 5) and have been accepted by a spiritual teacher" (*SH*, 602).

Indian sage (T: drang srong) is a holy hermit, hermit-saint, ṛṣi, Buddhist or non-Buddhist, such as a Brahmanical ascetic with magical powers, who is renowned for conduct and spiritual practice (*SH*, 270 n. 31; RY2).

inner heat (S: caṇḍālī; T: gtum mo) is a Vajrayāna term for a kind of mystic inner heat that comes about through performing certain tantric practices. The purpose of developing and experiencing this heat is to burn up one's obstacles and confusion.

Kadampa (T: Bka' gdams pa) school was the first new school to form in the period of the Later Transmission. It was based on Atiśa's teachings and founded by Atiśa's disciple, Dromtön (T: 'Brom ston). Its followers were known for their monastic discipline, study, and development of compassion. Many of its major lineages and practices later became absorbed into the Gelukpa school.

karma (T: las; action) is a law of causality central to Buddhism. According to the doctrine of cause and effect, every action one takes determines one's future conditions, whether in this or future lives, so that a wholesome action leads to better circumstances, and an unwholesome action leads to negative consequences. For more about karma, including its place in the Hindu and Jain religions, see *EB*, 415–17; *WE*, 226–37.

learning, contemplating, and meditating (T: thos bsam sgom gsum) is the process of three stages in the development of wisdom, prajñā. One should "listen" to the teachings by studying extensively. Then one should reflect upon them, using one's own intelligence. Finally, one should go into long retreats to have experiential realizations related to the teachings. *See EB*, 861–62; *WE*, 90–91.

Lobzang Dragpa, or **Tsongkhapa** (1357–1419; T: Blo bzang grags pa, Tsong kha pa) formed the main ideas and practices that came to characterize the Gelukpa school by bringing together exoteric and esoteric aspects of the Buddhist tradition, founding the Great Prayer festival in Lhasa, founding Ganden monastery near Lhasa in 1409, and so on. The other two main Gelukpa monasteries in Lhasa were founded by his direct disciples soon afterwards. *See EB*, 861–62, 215–16.

lower three realms (T: ngan song gsum) are those of hell beings, hungry ghosts, and animals.

Madhyamaka (T: Dbu ma; the Middle Way school) was one of the most influential philosophical systems of Indian Buddhism, and was developed on the basis of Nāgārjuna's writings, which explicated the Second Turning teachings of the *Prajñāpāramitā*, or Perfection of Wisdom literature on emptiness. Its name, Middle Way, refers to the middle way between the extremes of eternalism and nihilism.

Mahāmudrā (T: Phyag rgya chen po; Great Gesture or Great Seal) is a Vajrayāna transmission on the nature of mind and the union of emptiness and luminosity. These teachings trace back to Saraha (8th century), and were brought to Tibet by Marpa, retrospectively considered one of the forefathers of the Kagyü sect. *See also EB,* 488–89.

mahāsiddha (T: grub chen; great master of spiritual accomplishment, great adept) is a practitioner who is considered to be a realized master of tantric meditation. The term is applied especially to Indian Vajrayāna practitioners, many of whom lived between the eighth and the twelfth centuries. *See* James B. Robinson, trans., *Buddha's Lions: The Lives of The Eighty-Four Siddhas* (Berkeley, Calif.: Dharma Publishing, 1979); Keith Dowman, ed., trans., *Masters of Mahāmudrā: Songs and Histories of the Eighty-Four Siddhas* (Albany: State University of New York Press, 1985); *EB*, 490–91; and siddhi, below.

mamo (= T, or 'jig rten ma mo) is one of the eight kinds of lha sin (T: lha srin), semi-divine beings who can act as protectors of the Dharma (RY2).

mantra (T: sngags) is a Sanskrit syllable or combination of syllables with no translatable meaning; there are many different types of mantras with different purposes. Some symbolize a specific meditational deity and are used with the aim of evoking him or her, thereby leading to purification and realization. One accompanies recitations of a mantra with a certain posture and visualizations.

meditative equipoise (T: mnyam par bzhag, mnyam par 'jog, mnyam gzhag) is resting, composing, or settling the mind in meditation.

Milarepa (1040–1123; T: Mi la ras pa; the cotton-clad Mila, his clan name) is a famed and much-loved yogi and song-writer who is believed to have become enlightened in one lifetime as a result of intense dedication, perseverance, and mastery of meditations. Retrospectively considered a forefather of the Kagyü lineage, he was a crucial link in the transmission of teachings which his teacher, Marpa (Mar pa Chos kyi blo gros, 11th century), brought from India, including Mahāmudrā and the practice of yogic inner heat (T: gtum mo). (*See also* Mahāmudrā and inner heat.) From about the beginning of the sixteenth century on, Milarepa's life (T: rnam thar) and songs (mgur ma) were generally known from Tsang Nyön Heruka's (T: Gtsang smyon He ru ka's) fifteenth century compilation of each of them. For these, see Lobsang P. Lhalungpa, trans., *The Life of Milarepa* (Boston: Shambhala, 1985); Gtsang smyon He ru ka, comp., *Rnal 'byor gyi dbang phyug chen po mi la ras pa'i rnam mgur* (Xining: Mtsho sngon mi rigs dpe skrun khang, 1999); and Garma C. C. Chang, ed., trans., *The Hundred Thousand Songs of Milarepa*, 2 vols. (Boston: Shambhala, 1989).

Mind Training (T: Blo sbyong) is a group of Mahāyāna systems of mental discipline for purifying the mind. It was brought to Tibet by Atiśa, became renowned in the Kadampa school, and is still in widespread use today in all schools. *See PH* for a description of specific mind training practices.

Mt. Meru or **Mt. Sumeru** (T: Ri rab) is a mountain which is positioned, according to cosmology, as the axis of the world. Various large and small continents, lakes, and oceans are arranged around it.

nāga (T: klu) is a snake-like being thought to live in the underworld and water. The leader of the nāgas is a bodhisattva, and he resides in Lake Kokonor. For the pre-Buddhist origin of nāgas as symbols of water and fertility in India, see *EB*, 234, 466–67.

nirmāṇakāya (T: sprul pa'i sku) is an expression of dharmakāya in a visible, physical form taken for the purpose of guiding sentient beings. For example, the historical Buddha Śākyamuni is thought to be a nirmāṇakāya Buddha. For more, see *BT*, 55–78.

Nirvana (T: mya ngan las 'das pa; to blow out, extinguish; becoming extinguished) is the state that results after eliminating false ideas and conflicting emotions. The term is understood differently according to the Hīnayāna (= Śrāvakayāna) and the Mahāyāna. For the Hīnayāna practitioner, whose highest ideal is the level of arhat, nirvana is freedom from rebirth in cyclic existence. For the Mahāyāna practitioner, "nonlocalizable" nirvana is freedom from both the extreme of samsara and the extreme of the arhat's nirvana.

Oral or Hearing Lineage (T: Snyan brgyud) is the lineage of direct, oral, usually very secret transmissions passed from teacher to disciple, as opposed to the written material.

Padmasaṃbhava (=S), known in Tibetan as **Pema Jungne** (T: Pad ma 'byung gnas) or **Guru Rinpoche**, was the tantric master who is said to have been invited to Tibet by its king in the eighth century in order to tame indigenous spirits who were opposing Buddhism as a foreign religion and blocking the construction of the first Tibetan monastery, Samye (T: Bsam yas). After Padmasaṃbhava converted the local spirits into protectors of Buddhism, Samye was established without mishap. He gave many Vajrayāna teachings, and left other Vajrayāna teachings hidden as treasure texts, known as terma (gter ma),which were to be discovered later. He is considered the second Buddha by the Nyingmapa school, which regards him as its founder. For more, see *EB*, 623–25; Ye shes mtsho rgyal, *The Life and Liberation of Padmasaṃbhava*, 2 vols. (Emeryville, Calif.: Dharma Publishing, 1978).

Practice Lineage (T: sgrub brgyud) is the lineage of putting teachings into practice in contrast to focusing on the explication of the teachings (bshad brgyud).

Precious Ones (T: dkon mchog) or **Three Jewels** (T: dkon mchog gsum) are the three objects of refuge, the Buddha, Dharma and Saṅgha.

Pure Realm. *See* Buddha-field, above.

refuge. One takes refuge in the Buddha, the Dharma, and the Saṅgha to become free from the suffering of samsara. When one takes refuge, it means that one accepts Buddhism and the teachings as one's path. One embarks on an active process of causing the three objects of refuge to be generated within oneself. In tantric Buddhism, the lama is regarded as the essence of all three, Buddha, Dharma, and Saṅgha, as well as the essence of all the deities.

repa (T: ras pa) signifies one who wears cotton, and calls to mind yogis who wear cotton in the winter, keeping themselves warm with practices involving inner heat. The "repa" in Milarepa's name has this origin.

root lama (T: rtsa ba'i bla ma) is a tantric master who gives one the empowerments, reading transmissions, and/or the teachings that form the core of one's practice. One can have various root lamas of these different types.

samādhi (T: ting nge 'dzin, ting 'dzin) is one of the three trainings of Dharma along with those of moral discipline and wisdom. Samādhi refers to a family of techniques that includes meditative absorption, a deep calm, and intense concentration or contemplation, done with the aim of attaining an accurate and clear view of the way things are. Because samādhi is nondualistic, one has no experience of discrimination between self and others. For more on meditation, see *EB*, 520–30; *WE*, 88–90.

Samantabhadra (T: Kun tu bzang po) in this context is the primordial dharmakāya Buddha. I quote M. Ricard: "In the primordial universal ground, there are neither sentient beings, nor Buddhas; neither ignorance, nor enlightenment. It is a state of natural, unchanging perfection beyond conditions and concepts. When the first manifestation of phenomena arises from the primordial ground, to recognize that this arising is the display of one's own awareness leads instantaneously to the primordial Buddhahood of Samantabhadra. Not recognizing this to be the case, and taking phenomena and beings to be real entities distinct from oneself, leads instantaneously to the ignorance of sentient beings" (*SH*, 11, n. 3). Samantabhadra is also the name of a bodhisattva who is renowned as the speaker of the Praṇidhānarāja.

sambhogakāya (T: longs spyod rdzogs pa'i sku) is a body of perfect enjoyment, which is in a semi-manifest form and is only perceptible to bodhisattvas. It "represents the primary manifestation of dharmakāya, perfectly embodying the non-duality of appearance and emptiness" (*EB*, 78). *See also BT*, 54–55.

samsara (T: 'khor ba; wandering) in contrast to Nirvana, or liberation, is cycles of birth and death within the realms of sentient beings (gods, jealous gods, human beings, animals, tormented spirits, and hell beings). Being in samsara involves suffering because one still has attachments, aggression, and ignorance. They, in turn, again cause one to take another rebirth in the six realms.

Saṅgha (T: dge 'dun; community) are generally the followers of Buddhism, and more specifically, monks and nuns.

seven noble riches (T: 'phags pa'i nor bdun) are the riches of faith, discipline, learning, diligence or a sense of ethical conscience in regard to oneself, modesty, generosity, and intelligence (RY1; *SH*, 601).

seven postures of Vairocana (T: rnam snang chos bdun) are adopted during meditation. They are sometimes described as "the legs in full lotus, the spine straight, the shoulders broadened, the neck slightly bent, the hands in the gesture of equanimity, the tip of tongue touching the palate, and the gaze placed in the direction of the nose" (RY1). *See also EB*, 520–21.

siddha (T: grub thob; adept) is a tantric practitioner who is considered to be enlightened and to have accomplished the siddhis.

siddhi (T: dngos grub) is an accomplishment. The siddhis are traditionally divided into two groups: the **eight** mundane, or **common accomplishments** (T: thun mong gi dngos grub) are the development of powers: the siddhis of the sword, of pills, of eye medicine, of swift walking, of partaking of essences or alchemy, of being able to go to a celestial realm, of invisibility, and of underground treasure (ral gri'i dngos grub, ril bu, mig sman, rkang mgyogs, bcud len, mkha' spyod, mi snang ba, sa 'og) (IW1, RY1, JV). Some of these accomplishments have been explained in simple terms as "clairvoyance, clairaudience, flying in the sky, becoming invisible, everlasting youth, or powers of transmutation" (RY1). The development of these powers is a result of meditation. They are not meant to be goals in themselves. The **supreme accomplishment** (T: mchog gi dngos grub) is complete enlightenment. For further information on the common and supreme siddhis, and how the common ones relate to the supreme one, see Dowman, *Masters of Mahāmudrā*, 4–7.

six pāramitās or perfections (T: phar phyin, pha rol tu phyin pa; to reach the other shore) are central to the bodhisattva path. They are generosity, discipline, patience, effort, contemplation, and transcendental knowledge or insight. Unlike ordinary generosity and so on, they are pure actions untainted by attachment and free from dualistic concepts. The bodhisattva's ideal of compassion embraces the first five perfections. The last one is the bodhisattva's wisdom. For more, see *BT*, 35–38.

Sukhāvatī (T: Bde ba can) is the western pure Buddha-field of Buddha Amitābha. For a description of this blissful paradise, with its beautiful gardens and groves, see *EB*, 704. *See also* Buddha-field, above.

ten bhūmis (T: sa bcu) are stages that a bodhisattva goes through to reach enlightenment. At the end of the ten bhūmis, one arrives at the eleventh, perfect enlightenment. (There are ten levels before enlightenment in the sutra tradition, and thirteen levels before enlightenment in the tantric tradition.) For more, see *BT*, 17–28.

ten directions (T: phyogs bcu) are north, south, east, west, southeast, southwest, northeast, northwest, up, and down. This basically means "everywhere."

three bodies (S/E: three kāyas; T: sku gsum) of Buddha is a basic Mahāyāna doctrine and a means of understanding enlightened beings and their manifestations. *See* nirmāṇakāya, dharmakāya, sambhogakāya. For more on the three bodies, or kāyas, see *EB*, 76–79.

three kindnesses. There are two sets. Within the context of the sutras (T: mdo phyogs), they are giving precepts (sdom pa), reading authorizations (lung), and teachings of the sutra tradition (khrid). Within the context of the tantras (sngags phyogs) they are conferring empowerment (dbang bskur), explaining the tantras (rgyud bshad), and giving concise instructions of the tantric tradition (man ngag gnang ba).

three skills (T: rtsal gsum) are the power to make a small jump with great precision (T: tshad 'dzin thun ba'i rtsal), the power to make a long jump (ring bar bsgangs pa'i rtsal), and the power to move through space (bar snang du spar ba'i rtsal) (JV).

tsa, lung, thigle (S: nāḍī, prāṇa, bindu; T: rtsa, rlung, thig le) are often translated as channels, energies, and drops, respectively. According to Tibetan anatomy, life-supporting energies and drops flow through the channels. Meditating on these three allows a yogi to reverse the currents that draw his mind to objects, so the mind does not stir. The first of the six yogas of Nāropa, the generation of inner heat, involves exercises with the channels, energies, and drops. The heat is thought to melt the drops, which then flow in the channels and induce great bliss. *See also* inner heat, above.

true meaning. *See* definitive meaning, above.

truth body. *See* dharmakāya, above.

turn the wheel of the Dharma (T: chos 'khor skor ba) means to teach the Dharma. The Buddha's teachings have been given in three turnings.

two accumulations (T: tshogs gnyis) are merit (T: bsod nams), and wisdom (ye shes). Merit involves concepts, and wisdom is beyond concepts.

two bodies of Buddha (S/E: two kāyas; T. sku gnyis) are the dharmakāya and the rūpakāya. **Rūpakāya**, or **form bodies** (S/E: form kāyas; T: gzugs sku) include both the sambhogakāya and nirmāṇakāya, i.e. the bodies that have perceptible forms. *See also* three bodies, nirmāṇakāya, dharmakāya, sambhogakāya.

two purposes or benefits (T: don gnyis) are benefit for oneself (T: rang don), and benefit for others (gzhan don).

vajra body (T: rdo rje'i sku/ lus) is made up of tsa, lung, and thigle. *See* tsa, lung, thigle, above.

vajra brothers (T: rdo rje spun) are fellow practitioners who receive the same tantric initiations from the same lama (*TTC*).

Vajrasattva (T: Rdo rje sems dpa') is the sambhogakāya Buddha and lord of the five Buddha families. He is the Buddha of purification practices.

Victorious Ones (T: rgyal ba) is an epithet for the Buddhas, who have conquered samsara. The **sons of the Victorious Ones** (T: rgyal ba'i sras) are bodhisattvas.

victory banner (T: rgyal mtshan) is one of the eight auspicious symbols.

Vinaya (T: 'dul ba) are teachings of proper conduct and the literary sources for them. The teachings go back to nearly the beginning of Buddhism. They include precepts that should be observed by lay persons (7), by monks (252), and by nuns (320). These teachings of what to accept and what to reject comprise one of the three major groups of Buddhist teachings—Vinaya, Sutra, and Abhidharma. For more detail, see *EB*, 885–89.

wish-fulfilling cow (T: 'dod 'jo'i ba) is a magical cow that gives one all the milk one wants, and a metaphor for abundance.

yidam (= T), or tutelary deity, is one's personal meditation deity. As an embodiment of enlightened qualities, it is the object of one's meditation.

Sources for the Songs

I am listing the songs here by first line and page number, followed by the respective sources upon which my translations are based. I wish to thank Blo bzang chos grags, one of the great scholars of Reb gong, for his tireless effort in proofreading the Tibetan script provided in this book, and for suggesting some spelling deviations from previously published sources. I have adopted most of Blo bzang chos grags' suggestions and have inserted them into the text. I indicate the spelling changes below under the first lines of the songs by giving my spelling, the page and line number in this book; and the spelling, volume, and page number in the 2002 Xining edition of the *Gsung 'bum*.

Chapter 1. Lamas

Like the silver mist that rises: 4–5; *Gsung 'bum* 4: 330–31.

I pray to Ngawang Lobzang Tendzin: 8–11; *Gsung 'bum* 3: 639–40.

The cubs of the powerful snow lioness: 12–15; *Gsung 'bum* 3: 796.

Because I saw trees and flowers: 16–17; *Gsung 'bum* 3: 509.
grag in *Songs of Shabkar*: 16, line 6; *grags* in *Gsung 'bum* 3: 509.

Chapter 2. Impermanence

I bow to the guru. / A soft, pleasant rain...: 22–23; *Gsung 'bum* 3: 148.

I bow to the guru. / My lama Chökyi Gyälpo: 26–29; *Gsung 'bum* 4: 201.

Chapter 3. Passing Away of Mother and Father

Lord lama—Buddha—please dwell on my crown *cakra*: 32–37; *A ma dran pa'i mgur*, ff.: 545–47.

Before, when mother was alive, I did not want to see her: 40–43; *A ma dran pa'i mgur*, ff. 548–49.

Noble, Great Compassionate One, please hear my prayer: 44–55; *Gsung 'bum* 4: 149–52.
sdig in *Songs of Shabkar*: 52, line 1; *sdigs* in *Gsung 'bum* 4: 151.
bsgrubs in *Songs of Shabkar*: 54, line 2; *bsgrub* in *Gsung 'bum* 4: 152.

Chapter 4. Nature

Like an eagle that soars in the lofty blue heights: 58–61; *Gsung 'bum* 4: 503–4.

Tree branches—you are shaking and moving around so much: 62–63; *Gsung 'bum* 4: 410–11.
'khrug in *Songs of Shabkar*: 62, line 4; *'khrig* in *Gsung 'bum* 4: 411.

When flowers on the lush trees: 66–69; *Gsung 'bum* 4: 236–37.
tshe in *Songs of Shabkar*: 66, line 8; *che* in *Gsung 'bum* 4: 236.

When the water of faith and respect: 72–75; *Gsung 'bum* 3: 224–25.

Chapter 5. Death

I pray to the precious, qualified lama: 78–83; *Gsung 'bum* 3: 647–48.
bsam in *Songs of Shabkar*: 82, line 11; *gsum* in *Gsung 'bum* 3: 648.
gzhan in *Songs of Shabkar*: 82, line 13; *bzhin* in *Gsung 'bum* 3: 648.

In the beginning, I listened to and contemplated the Dharma in the presence of a lama: 86–89; *Gsung 'bum* 4: 770–71.

'The grove of crimson lotuses: 90–91; *Gsung 'bum* 4: 479–80.

The cub of the white lion: 92–93; *Gsung 'bum* 4: 823.

Chapter 6. Renunciation

At first, wealth was my happiness: 98–101; *Gsung 'bum* 3: 29–30.

I pray to the lord Milarepa: 102–7; *Gsung 'bum* 4: 207–8.

I pray to you, kind lamas: 108–11; *Gsung 'bum* 4: 419–20.
sgrub in *Songs of Shabkar*: 108, line 13; *bsgrub* in *Gsung 'bum* 4: 420.

I pray to Pema Jungne of Ogyen: 114–17; *Gsung 'bum* 3: 740–41.

Chapter 7. Old Age

Elderly father, Chökyi Gyälpo: 120–23; *Gsung 'bum* 4: 782.
po in *Songs of Shabkar*: 120, line 12; *bo* in *Gsung 'bum* 4: 782.
pa in *Songs of Shabkar*: 122, colophon; *pa* in *Gsung 'bum* 4: 782.

Rain and snow both: 126–29; *Gsung 'bum* 4: 480–81.
rtogs in *Songs of Shabkar*: 128, line 8; *rtog* in *Gsung 'bum* 4: 481.

You established the ripening and liberation of those to be tamed in this realm: 130–33; *Gsung 'bum* 4: 324–25.
bu in *Songs of Shabkar*: 130, line 12; *bur* in *Gsung 'bum* 4: 324.
ma in *Songs of Shabkar*: 130, line 14; *mas* in *Gsung 'bum* 4: 325.

Chapter 8. Self-Criticism

Oh father Chökyi Gyäl, possessed of the three kindnesses: 136–43; *Gsung 'bum* 3: 39–41.

Chapter 9. Nonsectarianism

I bow to the lama: 146–49; *Gsung 'bum* 4: 322–23.

Shining with radiant clarity, the sun rose: 150–53; *Gsung 'bum* 4: 323–24.
Songs of Shabkar: 150, line 12: I have omitted the syllable "*de*" in *Gsung 'bum* 4: 323, in order to maintain the meter.
thim in *Songs of Shabkar*: 152, line 6; *thum* in *Gsung 'bum* 4: 324.

I'm going, I'm going, I'm going to a solitary meadow: 156–59; *Gsung 'bum* 3: 208–9.

Chapter 10. Hermitage

They have wandered around mountain hermitages like the sun and moon: 162–69; *Gsung 'bum* 3: 106–8.

Oh yeah! The hunter, leading a dog, has arrived: 172–75; *Gsung 'bum* 3: 465.

The hunter, leading a dog, arrived: 178–81; *Shar skal ldan rgya mtsho'i mgur 'bum* (Xining: Mtsho sngon mi rigs dpe skrun khang, 1994): 160–61. Please note that this song is by Skal ldan rgya mtsho.

Precious, kind lama: 182–85; *Gsung 'bum* 3: 223–24.
wa'i in *Songs of Shabkar*: 182, line 7; *ba'i* in *Gsung 'bum* 3: 223.
gos in *Songs of Shabkar*: 184, line 12; *dgos* in *Gsung 'bum* 3: 224.

I bow at the feet of all scholars and siddhas: 188–95; *Gsung 'bum* 3:104–6.
bsgrengs in *Songs of Shabkar*: 188, line 3; *bsgreng* in *Gsung 'bum* 3:104.
thang in *Songs of Shabkar*: 190, line 7; *thad* in *Gsung 'bum* 3:105.

Chapter 11. Meditation Experiences

I bow at the feet of the elderly father, Chögyäl Ngakyi Wangpo: 198–99; *Gsung 'bum* 3: 730.

Your mind, like the sky, is empty and vast: 200–3; *Gsung 'bum* 4: 389–90.

The guru: 206–9; *Gsung 'bum* 4: 373.

I bow to Chökyi Gyälpo: 210–13; *Gsung 'bum* 3: 480–81.
rig in *Songs of Shabkar*: 210, line 5; *rigs* in *Gsung 'bum* 3: 481.

E ma! Joyous, clear awareness: 216–21; *Gsung 'bum* 4: 455–57.
yi in *Songs of Shabkar*: 218, line 6; *yis* in *Gsung 'bum* 4: 456.

Just as a skilled horseman: 222–25; *Gsung 'bum* 4: 561–62.

Chapter 12. Happiness

The three months of summer have arrived: 228–29; *Gsung 'bum* 3: 141.

I bow to the father, Chögyäl Ngakyi Wangpo: 232–35; *Gsung 'bum* 3: 490–91.

With no enemies at all to tame: 238–43; *Gsung 'bum* 3: 395–96.

Having prostrated myself with great respect: 246–49; *Gsung 'bum* 4: 512–13.

I bow respectfully to Chökyi Gyälpo: 250–51; *Gsung 'bum* 4: 374–75.

I prostrate myself to the guru: 254–55; *Gsung 'bum* 3: 174.

Chapter 13. Singing

I bow to the guru. / When you, the turquoise...: 258–59; *Gsung 'bum* 3: 111.
dbyangs in *Songs of Shabkar*: 258, line 12; *dbyangs* in *Gsung 'bum* 3: 111.

Above, my root and lineage lamas' blessings: 260–61; *Gsung 'bum* 4: 595–96.
D'a ki in *Songs of Shabkar*: 260, line 13; *DAkki* in *Gsung 'bum* 4: 596.

I bow to the guru. / In the wondrous grove: 262–67; *Gsung 'bum* 4: 545–46

I bow to the guru. / If the turquoise blue...: 270–71; *Gsung 'bum* 3: 148.

I bow to the guru. /The seasons of winter...: 272–75; *Gsung 'bum* 4: 243–44.
mnyam in *Songs of Shabkar*: 274, line 12; *nyams* in *Gsung 'bum* 4: 243.

Oh: 278–79; *Gsung 'bum* 3: 160–61.

An exact copy of a statue of Shabkar, said to have been made during his life and to look exactly like him. It shows him singing *gur* with the same *mudra* as Milarepa. This replica. about a foot and a half high, is on permanent display at the Jokhang at Yama Tashikhyil, and the precious statue itself is shown once a year on the 15th day of the 4th Tibetan month, at which time many people come to pay their respects.

The *gurdong* (T: *mgur sdong*, lit. tree for *gur*) at Yama Tashikhyil and Shabkar's seat in front of it, where he is said to have often sung *gur*

Biography

Shabkar Tshogdruk Rangdrol was born in 1781 in Shohong Lakha in the Rebgong region of Amdo. When he was ten, he entered Shohong Lakha Ngagdra, and joined a community of Nyingmapa yogis. In 1794, he received *Dzogchen* teachings from Jampel Dorje. Later, he met his root teacher, Ngakyi Wangpo, a Mongolian king who had renounced the throne and become a Nyingmapa master. While his main practice was *Dzogchen*, he also received teachings from many Gelukpa teachers, and was known for his nonsectarianism. For several decades, Shabkar sought the most suitable retreats for solitary practice, across Tibet from east to west, including Tshonying (the island in Lake Kokonor), Machen, Tsari, and Kailash. He also visited Nepal, where he offered gold to cover the spire of the Bodhnath stupa. In 1828, when he was forty-seven, he returned to Amdo, and was in retreat principally at Yama Tashikhyil. He passed away in 1851. He was the first of a lineage of which the fourth is alive today. *See Mi sna*, 867; *Ming mdzod*, 1470; *SH*, xiii–xvi; TBRC. For wave upon wave of colorful details of Shabkar's life, see his entire autobiography, *ZH*, the first part of which has been translated into English in *SH*.

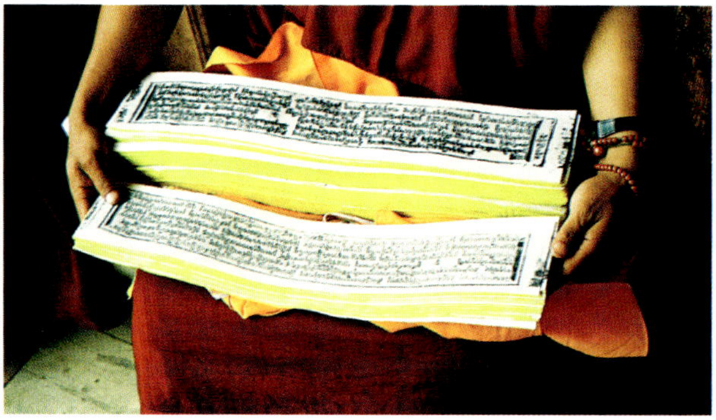

A Tibetan-style book or *pecha*, the *Collected Songs* of Milarepa, which had a strong influence on Shabkar

Victoria Sujata, also known as Ritröma Tashi Khandro, in White Horse Cave

Photo by Akhö Whanjor

Bibliography

Byang chub mi la Ngag dbang bsod nams. *Grub chen skal ldan rgya mtsho'i rnam thar yid bzhin dbang gi rgyal po*. Xining: Mtsho sngon mi rigs dpe skrun khang, 1990.

Chang, Garma C. C., ed., trans. *The Hundred Thousand Songs of Milarepa*. 2 vols. Boston: Shambhala, 1989.

Chögyam Trungpa. *Mudra: Early Poems & Songs*. Boston: Shambhala, 2001.

Cook, Elizabeth and the Yeshe De Project, under the direction of Tarthang Tulku. *The Buddha and His Teachings*. In *Crystal Mirror Series*. Vol. 10. Berkeley, Calif.: Dharma Publishing, 1995.

Delacour, Jean. *The Waterfowl of the World*. Vol. 1. London: Country Life, 1954.

[Dharma Publishing staff, under the guidance of Tarthang Tulku.] *Ways of Enlightenment: Buddhist Studies at Nyingma Institute*. Berkeley, Calif.: Dharma Publishing, 1993.

Don grub rgyal. *Bod kyi mgur glu byung 'phel gyi lo rgyus dang khyad chos bsdus par ston pa rig pa'i khye'u rnam par rtsen pa'i skyed tshal*. In *Dpal don grub rgyal gyi gsung 'bum*, by Don grub rgyal. Vol. 3, pp. 316–601. Beijing: Mi rigs dpe skrun khang, 1997.

Dowman, Keith, ed., trans. *Masters of Mahāmudrā: Songs and Histories of the Eighty-Four Buddhist Siddhas*. Albany: State University of New York Press, 1985.

Dowman, Keith and Sonam Paljor, trans. *The Divine Madman: The Sublime Life and Songs of Drukpa Kunley*. Clearlake, Calif.: The Dawn Horse Press, 1980.

Gtsang smyon He ru ka, comp. *Rnal 'byor gyi dbang phyug chen po mi la ras pa'i rnam mgur*. Xining: Mtsho sngon mi rigs dpe skrun khang, 1999.

Kunga Rimpoche, Lama and Brian Cutillo, trans. *Drinking the Mountain Stream: New Stories of Tibet's Beloved Saint, Milarepa*. Boston: Wisdom Publications, 1995.

_____. *Miraculous Journey: New Stories & Songs by Milarepa*. Novato, Calif.: Lotsawa, 1986.

Kvaerne, Per. *An Anthology of Buddhist Tantric Songs: A Study of the Caryāgīti*. Det Norske Videnskaps-Akademi. II. Hist.-Filos. Klasse. Skrifter, Ny Serie, no. 14. Oslo: Universitetsforlaget; Irvington-on-Hudson, N.Y.: Columbia University Press, 1977.

Lhalungpa, Lobsang P., trans. *The Life of Milarepa*. Boston: Shambhala, 1985.

Lopez, Donald S., Jr., ed., trans. *In the Forest of Faded Wisdom: 104 Poems by Gendun Chopel: A Bilingual Edition*. Chicago: The University of Chicago Press, 2009.

Mullin, Glenn H. *Mystical Verses of a Mad Dalai Lama*. Wheaton, Ill.: The Theosophical Publishing House, 1994.

Nālandā Translation Committee under the direction of Chögyam Trungpa, trans. *The Life of Marpa the Translator: Seeing Accomplishes All*. Boston: Shambhala, 1995.

_____. *The Rain of Wisdom: The Essence of the Ocean of True Meaning: The Vajra Songs of the Kagyü Gurus*. Boston: Shambhala, 1999.

Padma Gyurmed Namgyal, Zhechen Gyaltsab. *Path of Heroes: Birth of Enlightenment: With the Practice Instructions and Reflections of Tarthang Tulku*. Translated by Deborah Black. 2 vols. Berkeley, Calif.: Dharma Publishing, 1995.

Rabten, Geshe. *Song of the Profound View*. Edited and translated by Stephen Batchelor. London: Wisdom Publications, 1989.

Robinson, James B., trans. *Buddha's Lions: The Lives of the Eighty-Four Siddhas*. Berkeley, Calif.: Dharma Publishing, 1979.

Schaeffer, Kurtis R. *Dreaming the Great Brahmin: Tibetan Traditions of the Buddhist Poet-Saint Saraha*. New York: Oxford University Press, 2005.

Skal ldan rgya mtsho. *Shar skal ldan rgya mtsho'i mgur 'bum*. Xining: Mtsho sngon mi rigs dpe skrun khang, 1994.

Sørensen, Per K. *Divinity Secularized: An Inquiry into the Nature and Form of the Songs ascribed to the Sixth Dalai Lama*. Wiener Studien zur Tibetologie und Buddhismuskunde, heft 25. Wien: Arbeitskreis für tibetische und buddhistische Studien, Universität Wien, 1990.

Stearns, Cyrus, ed., trans. *Hermit of Go Cliffs: Timeless Instructions from a Tibetan Mystic*. Boston: Wisdom Publications, 2000.

Stein, R. A., ed., trans. *Vie et chants de 'Brug pa kun legs, le yogin*. Paris: G.-P. Maisonneuve et Larose, 1972.

Sujata, Victoria. "A Commentary on the *Mgur 'bum* (*Collected Songs of Spiritual Realization*) of Skal ldan rgya mtsho, a Seventeenth Century Scholar and Siddha from Amdo." Ph.D. diss., Harvard University, 2003.

_____. "Relationships between Inner Life and Solitary Places: The *Mgur* of Two *Siddhas* in Amdo." *Contributions to Tibetan Buddhist Literature: Proceedings of the Eleventh Seminar of the International Association for Tibetan Studies, Königswinter 2006*. Beiträge zur Zentralasienforschung. Halle: International Institute for Tibetan and Buddhist Studies, 2008.

_____. "The Singing of Seventeenth-Century *Mgur* in Amdo today: A Continuing Tradition." *Tibetan Studies: Proceedings of the Tenth Seminar of the International Association of Tibetan Studies, Oxford, 2003* (forthcoming).

_____. *Tibetan Songs of Realization: Echoes from a Seventeenth-Century Scholar and Siddha in Amdo*. Leiden: Brill, 2005.

Thrangu Rinpoche. *Songs of Nāropa*. Hong Kong: Rangjung Yeshe Publications, 1997.

Thupten Jinpa and Jaś Elsner, comps., trans. *Songs of Spiritual Experience: Tibetan Buddhist Poems of Insight & Awakening*. Boston: Shambhala, 2000.

Tsultrim Gyamtso Rinpoche, Khenpo. *Beautiful Song of Marpa the Translator*. Prajna Editions, inaugural issue. Auckland, New Zealand: Zhyisil Chokyi Ghatsal Publications, 2001.

Zhabs dkar Tshogs drug rang grol. *A ma dran pa'i mgur*. In *Zhabs dkar tshogs drug rang grol gyi bka' 'bum: The Collected Works of Zhabs dkar tshogs drug rang grol (1781–1851)*. Vol. 5 (Ca): 542–49. New Delhi: Shechen Publications, 2003.

_____. *Bya btang tshogs drug rang grol gyis rang dang skal ldan gdul bya la mgrin pa gdams pa'i bang mdzod nas glu dbyangs dga' ston 'gyed pa rnams*. In *Zhabs dkar tshogs drug rang grol gyi bka' 'bum: The Collected Works of Zhabs dkar tshogs drug rang grol (1781–1851)*. Vol. 3 (Ga), vol. 4 (Nga), and vol. 5 (Ca): 1–402. New Delhi: Shechen Publications, 2003.

_____. [*Bya btang tshogs drug rang grol gyis rang dang skal ldan gdul bya la mgrin pa gdams pa'i bang mdzod nas glu dbyangs dga' ston 'gyed pa rnams*.] In *Rje zhabs dkar tshogs drug rang grol gyi gsung 'bum*. Vols. 3–4. Xining: Mtsho sngon mi rigs dpe skrun khang, 2002.

_____. *Snyigs dus 'gro ba yongs kyi skyabs mgon zhabs dkar rdo rje 'chang chen po'i rnam par thar pa rgyas par bshad pa skal bzang gdul bya thar 'dod rnams kyi re ba skong ba'i yid bzhin gyi nor bu bsam 'phel dbang gi rgyal po*. In *Rje zhabs dkar tshogs drug rang grol gyi gsung 'bum* by Zhabs dkar Tshogs drug rang grol. Vol. 1. Xining: Mtsho sngon mi rigs dpe skrun khang, 2002.

_____. *Snyigs dus 'gro ba yongs kyi skyabs mgon zhabs dkar rdo rje 'chang chen po'i rnam par thar pa rgyas par bshad pa skal bzang gdul bya thar 'dod rnams kyi re ba skong ba'i yid bzhin gyi nor bu bsam 'phel dbang gi rgyal po*. In *Zhabs dkar tshogs drug rang grol gyi bka' 'bum: The Collected Works of Zhabs dkar tshogs drug rang grol (1781–1851)*. Vol. 1. New Delhi: Shechen Publications, 2003.

Zhabs dkar Tshogs drug rang grol, 1781–1851. *The Life of Shabkar: The Autobiography of a Tibetan Yogin*. Translated by Matthieu Ricard, et al. Albany: State University of New York Press, 1994.

_____. *Rainbows Appear: Tibetan Poems of Shabkar*. Edited and translated by Matthieu Ricard. Calligraphy by Jigme Doushe. Boston: Shambhala, 2002.

Websites

The Rangjung Yeshe Gilded Palace of Dharmic Activity: A Glossary of Buddhist People, Places, and Things. http://rywiki.tsadra.org/index.php/The_Rangjung_Yeshe_Gilded_Palace_of_Dharmic_Activity.

The Tibetan Buddhist Resource Center. E. Gene Smith, Executive Director. http://www.tbrc.org.

Discography

Sujata, Victoria, recorder, compiler, translator, and annotator. *Tibetan Songs of Realization: A Continuing Tradition from the Seventeenth Century*. CD. Brill, 2005. Available with Victoria Sujata, *Tibetan Songs of Realization: Echoes from a Seventeenth-Century Scholar and Siddha in Amdo* (Leiden: Brill, 2005).

Sources for Maps

Gyurme Dorje. *Footprint Tibet Handbook with Bhutan*. 2nd Edition. Bath, England: Footprint Handbooks, 1999.

Huber, Toni. "Introduction: A mdo and its Modern Transition." In *Amdo Tibetans in Transition: Society and Culture in the Post-Mao Era*. Edited by Toni Huber. Pp. xi–xxiii. Vol. 2/5 of Brill's Tibetan Studies Library: *PIATS 2000: Tibetan Studies: Proceedings of the Ninth Seminar of the International Association for Tibetan Studies, Leiden 2000*, ed., Henk Blezer. Brill: Leiden, 2002.

Osada, Yukiyasu, et al. *Mapping the Tibetan World*. Reprint. Reno, NV: Kotan Publishing, Inc., 2001.

Zhabs dkar Tshogs drug rang grol, 1781–1851. *The Life of Shabkar: The Autobiography of a Tibetan Yogin*. Translated by Matthieu Ricard, et al. Albany: State University of New York Press, 1994, maps 1–3.

Websites

Geographical Glossary from Matthieu Ricard. http://rywiki.tsadra.org/index.php/Geographical_Glossary_from_Matthieu_Ricard

Google Earth. earth.google.com

THL Place Dictionary in The Tibetan & Himalayan Library. http://places.thlib.org

A Note on the Maps

The maps in this book were created with ArcGIS software, using SRTM (= Shuttle Radar Topography Mission) data on topography and ESRI (=Environmental Sensitivities Research Institute) data on political boundaries, cities, and rivers for geographic reference. Smaller towns and monasteries not contained in the ESRI database were visually located using Google Earth (at earth.google.com) and added to the map by their geographic coordinates.

The ESRI database is in Chinese, whereas the names I was looking for are in Tibetan. To solve this problem, I consulted various guidebooks for the name of a nearby Chinese town, the same information that a traveler may need to know in order to arrive at a destination in Amdo or other regions inhabited indigenously by Tibetans within China, where the drivers are often Han Chinese or Moslem. I then entered the coordinates of the nearby town into Google Earth, and followed the guidebook's directions to the desired place by following the roads via satellite images (or by memory if I had been there) in order to arrive at the desired place for my map and determine its coordinates. Hence, the process of attempting to pinpoint the exact locations differed from place to place, and though my main sources were the ESRI database and Google Earth, I sometimes supplemented them with other sources, included in my bibliography above.

The largest challenge I faced was locating the region of Amdo itself, generally described as being on the northeastern side of the Tibetan plateau, mostly in the present-day Chinese province of Qinghai, with smaller portions in Gansu and Sichuan. Attempts to be more specific describe the location of Amdo's borders in various ways, such as by mountain ranges (*Tibet Handbook,* 507); and by rivers, towns, and a stupa (M. Ricard, ryriki). Amdo has been described as a collection of various modern counties (*Tibet Handbook,* maps 1 and 5), and as the area where Amdo Tibetans live, and the Tibetan Autonomous Prefectures that they inhabit (Huber, xiii–xiv). Huber furthermore points out that though every Tibetan thinks he knows where Amdo is, the accounts usually differ, as do written sources. "There is not, and there has never been, a single or discrete Amdo in time and space... The only certainty we can entertain is that the area referred to as Amdo by Tibetans today must include those parts of the northeastern Tibetan plateau where people regard themselves as being ethnically Tibetan ...." (Huber, xiii). The region Rebgong has also been defined in various ways over time. In the present, it is almost equivalent to the modern Tongren *xian*, one of the four counties in Huangnan prefecture. Hence I have estimated the position of Amdo for map 1 and Rebgong for map 2 without putting borders around them. Yet when one is there, both Amdo and Rebgong feel like very clearly definable regions.

My most startling experience in creating these maps was to discover that I could use Google Earth to see clearly the rooftops of Rongbo Tashikhyil monastery, Kälden Gyatso's forest hermitage, and the surrounding, very stark mountainous terrain at 35° 35′40.55″ N 101° 59′16.04″ E. Unfortunately the area to the east of Rongbo valley, including Yama Tashikhyil, is presently still very fuzzy. Once Google Earth updates this portion of its photos, I assume that we will be able to enjoy views of the roofs of the monastery of the present day from satellite photos, and "fly" there also, at whim.

Table of Tibetan Words

Phonetics	*Transliteration*
Amdo	A mdo
Amnye Machen	Aa myes rma chen
Arig	A rig
Chenrezig	Spyan ras gzigs
Chögyäl Ngakyi Wangpo	Chos rgyal Ngag gi dbang po
Chökyi Gyälpo	Chos kyi rgyal po
Dönyö Phüntsog	Don yod phun tshogs
Dzogchen	*Rdzogs chen*
Ganden	Dga' ldan
Gelukpa	Dge lugs pa
gur	*mgur*
Gurbum	*Mgur 'bum*
gurdong	*mgur sdong*
gurma	*mgur ma*
Jampel Dorje	'Jam dpal rdo rje
Jamyang Gyatso	'Jam dyangs rgya mtsho
Jokhang	Jo khang
Kadampa	Bka' gdams pa
Kälden Gyatso	Skal ldan rgya mtsho
Labrang Tashikhyil	Bla brang Bkra shis 'khyil
Legnye	*Legs nyes*
Lhasa	Lha sa
Lobzang Dragpa	Blo bzang grags pa
Lobzang Rinchen	Blo bzang rin chen
Machen	Rma chen
Magyäl	Rma rgyal
Mahādeva	Ma ha'a de ba

Marpa	Mar pa
Milarepa	Mi la ras pa
Mindroling	Smin grol gling
Ngawang Lobzang Tendzin	Ngag dbang blo bzang bstan ʼdzin
Nyingmapa	Rnying ma pa
Ogyen	O rgyan
pecha	*dpe cha*
Pema Jungne	Padma ʼbyung gnas
Pema Karpo	Padma dkar po
Rebgong	Reb gong
ritröma	*ri khrod ma*
Rongbo	Rong bo
Rongbo Tashikhyil	Rong bo Bkra shis ʼkhyil
Sangye Dongrub	Sangs rgyas don grub
Shabkar Tshogdruk Rangdrol	Zhabs dkar Tshogs drug rang grol
Shohong Lakha	Zho ʼong la kha
Shohong Lakha Ngagdra	Zho ʼong la kha sngags grwa
Tashi Khandro	Bkra shis mkha' 'gro
Tashikhyil	Bkra shis ʼkhyil
Thubten Gyatso	Thub bstan rgya mtsho
Thukje Chenpo	Thugs rje chen po
Tise	Ti se
Trishor Gyälmo	Khri shor rgyal mo
Tsang Nyön Heruka	Gtsang smyon He ru ka
Tsari	Tsaʼa ri
Tsho Ngönpo	Mtsho sngon po
Tshogdruk Rangdrol	Tshogs drug rang grol
Tshonying	Mtsho snying
Tsongkhapa	Tsong kha pa
Ugyen	U rgyan
Ütsang	Dbus gtsang
Yama Tashikhyil	G.ya ma Bkra shis ʼkhyil

Index